NATIONAL PORTRAIT GALLERY

ROYAL FACES

FROM WILLIAM THE CONQUEROR TO THE PRESENT DAY

DANA BENTLEY-CRANCH

LONDON:HMSO

© Copyright Controller of HMSO 1990
First edition published 1977
Second edition published 1990
ISBN 0 11 290464 5

British Library Cataloguing in Publication Data
A CIP catalogue record for this book is available from the British Library

HMSO publications are available from:

HMSO Publications Centre
(Mail and telephone orders only)
PO Box 276, London, SW8 5DT
Telephone orders 071-873 9090
General enquiries 071-873 0011
(queuing system in operation for both numbers)

HMSO Bookshops
49 High Holborn, London, WC1V 6HB 071-873 0011 (counter service only)
258 Broad Street, Birmingham, B1 2HE 021–643 3740
Southey House, 33 Wine Street, Bristol, BS1 2BQ (0272) 264306
9–21 Princess Street, Manchester, M60 8AS 061-834 7201
80 Chichester Street, Belfast, BT1 4JY (0232) 238451
71 Lothian Road, Edinburgh, EH3 9AZ 031-228 4181

HMSO's Accredited Agents
(see Yellow Pages)

and through good booksellers

Front cover: *top left* William the Conqueror depicted on the Bayeux Tapestry (Centre Guillaume le Conquérant, Bayeux); *bottom left* Elizabeth I, the Armada portrait (detail) by George Gower, *c.*1588 (National Portrait Gallery); *centre* Richard II, panel portrait, *c.*1395 (Dean and Chapter of Westminster); *top right* Henry VIII (detail) after Holbein, *c.*1536 (National Portrait Gallery); *bottom right* Queen Elizabeth II, 1988 (Dave Chancellor/ Alpha)
Back cover *left to right*: Charles II in coronation robes (detail), by John Michael Wright, 1661 (Royal Collection); Queen Victoria (detail) by Lady Julia Abercromby, after von Angeli, 1883 (National Portrait Gallery); The Queen Mother, 1970, by Cecil Beaton (Camera Press).

ROYAL HOUSES

HOUSE OF NORMANDY

William I	1066–1087
William II	1087–1100
Henry I	1100–1135
Stephen	1135–1154

HOUSE OF PLANTAGENET

Henry II	1154–1189
Richard I	1189–1199
John	1199–1216
Henry III	1216–1272
Edward I	1272–1307
Edward II	1307–1327
Edward III	1327–1377
Richard II	1377–1399

HOUSE OF LANCASTER

Henry IV	1399–1413
Henry V	1413–1422
Henry VI	1422–1461

HOUSE OF YORK

Edward IV	1461–1483
Edward V	1483
Richard III	1483–1485

HOUSE OF TUDOR

Henry VII	1485–1509
Henry VIII	1509–1547
Edward VI	1547–1553
Mary I	1553–1558
Elizabeth I	1558–1603

HOUSE OF STUART

James I	1603–1625
Charles I	1625–1649
INTERREGNUM	1649–1660
Charles II	1660–1685
James II	1685–1688
Mary II	1688–1694
William III	1688–1702
Anne	1702–1714

HOUSE OF HANOVER

George I	1714–1727
George II	1727–1760
George III	1760–1820
George IV	1820–1830
William IV	1830–1837
Victoria	1837–1901

HOUSE OF SAXE-COBURG

Edward VII	1901–1910

HOUSE OF WINDSOR

George V	1910–1936
Edward VIII	1936
George VI	1936–1952
Elizabeth II	1952–

ACKNOWLEDGEMENTS

The author and publisher are grateful to the following for permission to reproduce the illustrations which appear in this book:

Alpha Photographic Agency Ltd, London; Ashmolean Museum, Oxford; Centre Guillaume le Conquérant, Bayeux, Courtesy of the Ville de Bayeux; British Library, London; British Museum, reproduced by Courtesy of the Trustees of the British Museum, London; Camera Press, London; Conway Library, Courtauld Institute of Art, London; Office de Tourisme, Falaise; Garamond Publishers Ltd, London; Sonia Halliday and Laura Lushington, Weston Turville, Buckinghamshire; Imperial War Museum, London, TR 2835 Crown copyright; the Archbishop of Canterbury and the Trustees of Lambeth Palace Library, London; National Gallery, London; National Museums and Galleries on Merseyside, Walker Art Gallery, Liverpool; National Portrait Gallery, London; Photo Ellebé, Rouen; Public Record Office, London; The Royal Archives, Windsor Castle, by gracious permission of Her Majesty The Queen; The Royal Collection, St James's Palace, London, copyright reserved, reproduced by gracious permission of Her Majesty The Queen; The Royal Library, Windsor Castle, copyright 1990 Her Majesty The Queen; The Royal Photographic Society, Bath; St George's Chapel, Windsor Castle, by permission of the Dean and Canons of Windsor; Times Newspapers Ltd, London; Victoria & Albert Museum, London, Courtesy of the Board of Trustees of the V&A; Warburg Institute, London; Westminster Abbey, by courtesy of the Dean and Chapter of Westminster; Winchelsea Church, Winchelsea; Woodmansterne Ltd, Watford.

We are also grateful for permission to quote from the following:

words of Winston Churchill, courtesy of Curtis Brown, on behalf of the estate of Winston Churchill; G N Garmonsway (transl.) *The Anglo-Saxon Chronicle*, Everyman's Library, J M Dent & Sons Ltd, 1960; Elizabeth Hallam (gen. ed.), *The Plantagenet Chronicles*, first published by Weidenfeld & Nicholson, London, 1986, copyright Phoebe Phillips Editions/Garamond Publishers Ltd; By the gracious permission of Her Majesty The Queen: quotations from the letters and journals of Queen Victoria, King Edward VII, King George V, Queen Mary, King George VI and Queen Elizabeth The Queen Mother, held in the Royal Archives.

INTRODUCTION

'What did he, or she, look like?' This question has been asked through the ages and never with more interest than when the face is a royal one. But putting faces to names is only one facet of the story of 900 years of British monarchy, and gives rise to other questions: 'How did he, or she, attain the throne?', 'What was the line of succession?' and, ultimately: 'How did the absolutist rule of the early kings finally evolve into constitutional monarchy?'. This book traces the fate of the Crown, from the moment William the Conqueror leapt ashore and changed the course of history – that he slipped and had to grip a handful of English soil was considered a good omen by his followers – up to the present-day House of Windsor.

Threading one's way through the tangled fortunes of the Houses of Normandy, Plantagenet, Lancaster, York, Tudor, Stuart, Hanover, Saxe-Coburg and Windsor one becomes increasingly aware of the problem of the line of succession. In early days this ever-present anxiety was heightened by the fact that the Crown, the throne and the Royal Treasure were tangible objects and not abstract concepts. Chroniclers tell us that the Norman king Henry I literally seized the Treasure and hurried off to have himself crowned; that the Plantagenet king Henry II actually placed his crown on the head of his eldest son in an attempt to secure his dynastic succession; that, having deposed Richard II, the Lancastrian Henry IV dramatically displayed the empty throne to the assembled barons and then took possession of it; and that on Bosworth battlefield the gold circlet was triumphantly snatched from the helmet of the dead Yorkist

William the Conqueror acknowledges Harold's oath of allegiance. Scene from the Bayeux Tapestry

Richard III and placed on the head of the founder of the House of Tudor, Henry VII.

The widespread preoccupation with the line of descent of the crown is illustrated in the meticulous care which the founders of the early royal houses took to substantiate their claims and give them some appearance of legality. William the Conqueror announced that he had been 'designated' by King Edward the Confessor (as did Harold), and his son, William II, made the same claim in his turn. To 'designation' was soon added the notion of 'suitability', an important element in troubled times when kingship implied a strong, mature ruler and which became so well recognised that it is surprising to find it over-ridden by the determination to adhere only to the 'line of descent' in the case of the two child-kings of the Plantagenet House, Henry III and Richard II. When Henry IV placed his House of Lancaster on the throne, his claim, as grandson of Edward III, was ostensibly hereditary, as was that of the head of the House of York who ousted Henry's grandson. But after the destructive Wars of the Roses when the English people found the House of Tudor on the throne, the 'suitability' of Henry VII as a strong ruler able to bring peace and prosperity to an exhausted country took precedence over his somewhat weak and complicated hereditary claims.

King John's seal on the Magna Carta

Meanwhile, throughout these turbulent times a system of government was slowly taking shape. The Norman Conqueror's Domesday Book and the administrative restructuring undertaken by his son Henry I, the 'lion of justice', opened the way for the improvements by the 'father of the common law', Henry II, first of the Plantagenets. The misrule of the latter's son, John, led to what has come to be known as the foundation of English liberties, the Magna Carta. Sealed in 1215, it was re-issued many times, each time re-affirming that recognised procedures must be followed in all relations between king and subject. The reign of John's son, Henry III, was notable for an innovation introduced not by the king but by a subject – Simon de Montfort, briefly in charge during the king's imprisonment, summoned not only the barons, but knights to represent the shires and burgesses to represent the towns, to attend his 'parleyings', thus sowing the seed for future Parliaments. And Edward I, the supreme legislator who created the basis of modern land law, not only adopted

Edward III as 'Lord of the Sea'

Simon's innovation but introduced another by having all his statutes passed through Parliament. By the time Henry VII took over a country weary of disorder, the Crown was so strongly supported by the rising classes of country gentry and merchants, and the peerage so weakened by war, that he was able not only to fight off the claims of pretenders, but also to stabilise government, to extend his Council to include the 'rising' men and to leave his house more financially secure than any of its predecessors.

England, from being part of the Continental empires of first Norman and then Plantagenet monarchs, was slowly progressing towards a sense of national unity, a process in which language played a part. In Edward III's reign the French spoken by the ruling classes gave way to one language for all. In 1362 English became the official language of the law-courts, in the following year Parliament was opened for the first time by a Chancellor speaking in English, and in Edward's household his page, Geoffrey Chaucer, was growing up to become the author of the first major work written in vernacular English, the *Canterbury Tales*.

Henry VII.
Detail from a panel
painting by Sittow, 1505

Medieval monarchs gave little thought to the image of their royal face in life. Their appearance remains doubtful and enigmatic, frozen into the effigies on their tombs, on their coins, and in a handful of illuminated manuscripts and painted panels. But the universal preoccupation with death filled this gap, in dramatic fashion, with the established procedure of making funeral effigies. As soon as a monarch expired, a mask was taken from his face and, using this death-mask as a model, a wooden head was carved and attached to a wooden, wickerwork, or straw-stuffed body dressed in the robes of the dead monarch. (Henry V's effigy was made of *cuir bouilli* – leather hardened by boiling – presumably to ensure its survival during the three months that his funeral procession took to travel from France to Westminster Abbey). The resulting effigy lay in state during the protracted funeral arrangements, was placed on top of the coffin for the funeral procession, and after the ceremony was positioned on or near the vault until the permanent tomb-effigy was ready. Most of these ephemeral effigies of the early English kings and their queens crumbled to dust long ago, but the few that have survived afford surprisingly vivid glimpses of these otherwise unknown royal faces.

Funeral effigy
of Elizabeth of York,
wife of Henry VII

A new chapter in England's history began when her handsome young Renaissance prince, Henry VIII, was crowned in 1509. Building on the foundations laid by his careful father, and financially secure, Henry threw himself with zest into mastering the art of kingship. As his father had done, he filled his Council with the 'new men' whose entire loyalty was to the crown; his most eminent adviser, Cardinal Wolsey, was the son of an Ipswich butcher. At the height of his career Wolsey exercised unprecedented authority over Church and State, authority which was soon taken over by his observant master. Henry's break with the Church of Rome, which brought his country into the Reformation movement, coincided with a widespread dislike of Papal power. The remark of the Duke of Suffolk, Henry's brother-in-law – 'It was never merry in England when we had cardinals among us' – expressed the popular view. The notion that the king was henceforth supreme in every sphere of life, and that England was self-sufficient and subject to no outside authority, gained ground, reinforced by the Crown's deliberate cultivation of regal magnificence, dignity and grandeur; the mode of address to the monarch underwent a subtle change from 'Your Grace' (a form shared with archbishops and dukes) to the unique term 'Your Majesty'. These great changes produced, paradoxically enough, a stronger and more competent Parliament, since Henry relied on its support and cooperation. He himself declared, towards the end of his reign: 'We at no time stand so highly in our estate royal as in the time of Parliament'. Elizabeth I managed her Parliaments as skilfully as her father had learned to do, telling them early in her reign: 'You shall never have a more natural mother than I mean to be unto you all', and assuring her last Parliament: 'And though you have had, and may have, many mightier and wiser princes sitting in this seat, yet you never had, nor shall have, any that will love you better'.

The royal face sprang into life in the reign of Henry VIII, a monarch who understood and welcomed Renaissance trends and ideas. When Francis I of France acquired Clouet as his court painter the French mania for portraits, which England was soon to copy, was under way. In 1526 two miniatures arrived in England, presents from Francis, depicting his two sons held as hostages by the emperor. These miniatures, with their magnificent settings and above all their delicate and

Henry VIII,
after Holbein, c.1536

Elizabeth I.
Detail from the
'Pelican Portrait'
attributed to Hilliard,
c.1572–6

charming likenesses of the little boys, caused a sensation at Henry's court. Although these portraits were presented with the ulterior political motive of encouraging Henry to help in the release of the boys, the actual result was to galvanise him into cultural emulation. Quickly assimilating the immense power and potential of the portrait, he set the Hornebolte family, recently arrived from Ghent, to work. Lucas Hornebolte was to produce an impressive array of miniatures, or pictures 'in little', of royal faces. And in Holbein Henry found an artist who could achieve a striking likeness while representing the monarch as a powerful symbol of kingship. At the same time the 'line of descent' became visual; Holbein's great mural at Whitehall Palace demonstrated to contemporary viewers that the House of Tudor was firmly established on the throne. Henceforth the image of the royal face became an essential element of the sixteenth-century English court, fulfilling an increasing number of practical, rather than artistic, functions. Portraits of Henry VIII's son, the Protestant boy-king Edward VI, proliferating during the religious turmoils of the reign of his Catholic half-sister Mary, served as pledges of religious faith. The exchange of portraits between monarchs took on the significance of a diplomatic gesture, a recognised overture illustrated by Mary Queen of Scots' anxious enquiry to the English ambassador as to whether Elizabeth I would reciprocate her gift of a portrait: 'for I assure you that if I thought you would not send me hers she should not have mine'. Portraits were also distributed to loyal courtiers. In Elizabeth's reign the production of these images became part of government policy, embedded in statutes authorising official 'patterns' to be copied, and associating the queen's image with loyalty to the Crown.

Elizabeth's childlessness brought the House of Stuart onto the throne in 1603, and set in motion the long tussle between king and commons. Parliament's determination to have a say in the vexed questions of foreign policy and religious matters which the Stuart kings, like the Tudors before them, regarded as the royal prerogative, led to civil war and regicide. The eleven-year Interregnum, during which Oliver Cromwell failed to find a constitutional basis for his government, ended with his death. The newly-elected 'free' Parliament summoned by General Monk invited Charles II to ascend the throne of his father. The 'line of descent'

Edward VI.
Detail, artist unknown

Miniature of Charles I
as a boy, studio of Oliver

5

emerged unscathed with the re-instation of the House of Stuart, only to be again under threat when the belated arrival of a son for James II aroused dormant fears of a Catholic dynasty. Parliament transferred the crown to James's Protestant daughters, brought in a Bill of Rights to define relations between ruler and government, and in 1701 passed the Act of Settlement which eventually brought the House of Hanover onto the throne. By this time, the House of Commons was pre-eminent, political parties and cabinet government were taking shape and, in spite of any prerogative powers claimed by the crown, the absolute ruler had disappeared and the constitutional monarch of modern times was gradually evolving.

From the days of the House of Stuart onwards the 'line of descent' was conscientiously charted by state portraiture which soon settled into a predictable and conventional style. The increasingly sophisticated painted portrait was, however, still accompanied by the medieval funeral effigy. The habit of making these archaic images lingered on, although for a different, and commercial, purpose. Charles II's effigy, considered by his contemporaries to be 'to ye lyfe and truly to admiration', was displayed in a case beside his vault to a public paying a fee for this privilege to the gentlemen of the Westminster Abbey choir.

Many monarchs regarded sitting for their state portraits as a tiresome necessity, but several – notably Charles I, George III, George IV and Queen Victoria – were intensely interested in their personal iconography. By inducing Van Dyck to set up his studio in England, Charles I was instrumental in introducing a style of court portraiture which carried on unchanged during the Cromwellian Protectorate (when painters simply continued to 'do Vandikes') and remained fashionable for over a century. One of George III's favourite court painters, Zoffany, paid his tribute to his illustrious predecessor by portraying the monarch and his family in Van Dyck costumes. To George III's father, the art patron Frederick, Prince of Wales, who died without succeeding to the throne, should be given the credit of moving the royal faces, pictorially speaking, into an open-air setting for more informal portrayals, a trend followed by his son and by his grandson George IV, and by many later monarchs and their artists.

Queen Victoria combined her keen interest in the history and iconography of her ancestors and her con-

George I.
Detail from an oil
painting by Kneller, 1716

Queen Victoria.
Detail from a photograph
by Fenton, 1854

temporary relatives and her appreciative and generous commissions to artists, with her own talents as a water-colourist. She and Prince Albert also mastered the techniques of etching, a skill which for Albert conveniently allied art and science. The result was an unsurpassed panorama of Victoria's long reign, with every major event, many domestic details and all the royal faces faithfully recorded. To the oil paintings, miniatures, statues, medals, etchings and water-colours were soon added the products of the camera. The new 'art and science' of photography was eagerly welcomed by Victoria and Albert. They became joint patrons of the newly-formed Photographic Society and the first suggestion that the Society should establish a permanent collection of photographs came from the prince himself.

Early photographs, because of the slow procedure, congealed their subjects into the rigidity of painted portraiture. But in time photography opened up new perspectives, not only showing the face of royalty animated, lively and – unthinkable until then – actually laughing, but providing an almost day-by-day record. Through the medium of the camera today's public can follow the ongoing pictorial chronicle of the royal faces of tomorrow's king and queen, Prince Charles and Princess Diana, emblems of contemporary Britain.

Queen Elizabeth II and Prince Philip at Balmoral, 1976

Prince Charles and Princess Diana on a state visit to Cameroon, 1990

WILLIAM I
Born 1027, reigned 1066–1087

'1066: In this year came William and conquered England ...'. England had suffered many invasions before 1066, but the arrival in that year, recorded in the *Anglo-Saxon Chronicle*, of 'William the Conqueror', the Norman duke whose dynasty would occupy the throne of England for almost a hundred years, was a turning-point in her history.

When King Edward the Confessor died childless on 6 January 1066, the succession was uncertain, with three claimants to the throne: Edward's brother-in-law Harold of Wessex, leader of the army, first man in the kingdom and generally regarded as the 'under-king'; King Harold Hardrada of Norway; and Duke William of Normandy. The latter not only saw himself as Edward's choice, but considered that Harold of Wessex had previously forfeited his own claim by swearing a solemn oath, on the relics of Bayeux Cathedral, to support William's candidature. This mystifying incident is depicted on the famous Bayeux Tapestry made for Bishop Odo of Bayeux, William's half-brother.

In the event, Harold was crowned King of England on the day after Edward's death, and the other two claimants prepared to invade. Harold defeated and killed the King of Norway in a decisive battle at Stamford Bridge near York in late September. By 14 October he was facing William's invading Normans at Hastings and in the ensuing battle lost both Crown and life. William, taking his army on a long and roundabout march to London and harrying the countryside as he went, subdued opposition to such purpose that on Christmas Day 1066 he was crowned in Westminster Abbey.

William rewarded his Normans with lands of the English earls who had fallen at Hastings, and followed his usual military procedure of building castles, in the Norman stone motte-and-bailey style, in key positions – preparations rendered necessary by the outbreak of rebellions in Northumbria, Wessex and Mercia. Although some pockets of resistance remained – such as that of Hereward the Wake in the Fens – by 1070 most of England had been pacified and was beginning to feel the effects of the Norman Conquest, which had virtually made England a partner in an Anglo-French state, bringing her in close touch with the mainstream of European culture and customs. For the ruling classes language was no barrier in this partnership: Latin was the universal tongue of the upper clergy, and French the common language of the court and aristocracy in England and Normandy. As for the Channel, instead of being a dividing factor, it formed a communicating link in days when travelling by water was the easiest mode of transport.

William's strong administration – 'though stern beyond all measure to those who opposed his will, he was kind to all those good men who loved God' (*Anglo-Saxon Chronicle*) – wrought lasting changes in English society. During his customary 'crown-wearing' at Gloucester during Christmas 1085 (the crown was also worn at Winchester at Easter and at Westminster at Whitsun-side), the Conqueror took stock of his achievements. He had 'important deliberations and exhaustive discussions with his council about this land, and how it was peopled and with what sort of men. Then he sent his men all over England into every shire ... and by his foresight it was surveyed so carefully that there was not a 'hide [the measure of land needed to support one family and one fully equipped soldier] ... in England of which he did not know who held it and how much it was worth and these particulars he set down in his survey.' This survey, known to later generations as 'Domesday' because it was considered the final court of appeal in disputes on land tenure, forms impressive evidence of royal administration unparalleled in contemporary Europe and was probably compiled in just over a year. Its instigator may never have seen it – fighting to defend Normandy from French attacks, William died from injuries in September 1087 and was buried in Caen Cathedral, leaving the Crown of England to his second son William Rufus who succeeded him as William II.

Pictorial representation of royalty was unconcerned with the royal face; what mattered was to depict the crown on the

Statue of William the Conqueror erected in Falaise, his birthplace, in 1851.
OFFICE DE TOURISME, FALAISE

William I depicted on the Bayeux Tapestry.
CENTRE GUILLAUME LE CONQUÉRANT

royal head, all the more so in an age when 'seizing the Crown' was a literal and not merely a metaphorical act. The lively pictures of the Bayeux Tapestry depict the crown of England firmly on the heads of King Edward the Confessor and his successor, Harold, but have to rely on embroidered captions to identify Duke William. The thirteenth-century historian and artist-monk of St Albans, Matthew Paris, also made no attempt to portray the four kings of the House of Normandy – William I, his two sons William II and Henry I, and Henry's nephew Stephen – as anything other than stylised symbols of kingship.

The strong hand with which William the Conqueror ruled England was missing in his dealings with his three sons, who quarrelled with each other and their father during his lifetime and, after his death, bitterly disputed their inheritance. Robert, the eldest, was given the Duchy of Normandy; Henry, the youngest, was given money; while William Rufus, the second son, assumed the Crown of England and subjected the country to thirteen years of severe government, during which he crushed rebellions, flouted Church authority and imposed crippling taxes. As the *Anglo-Saxon Chronicle* recorded: 'he was very harsh and fierce in his rule over his realm . . . and very terrifying.

When temporarily in charge of Normandy, and while Duke Robert took part in the First Crusade, the king led a series of campaigns against the French. More were planned but, on 2 August 1100 while hunting in the New Forest, William Rufus was hit by an arrow – whether by accident or by design remains a mystery – and died immediately. The chronicler William of Malmesbury described the sequel: 'A few of the peasants carried his corpse to the cathedral at Winchester on a horse-drawn wagon, with blood dripping from it the whole way . . . '.

During the wagon's slow progress, Henry, William's younger brother who had been a member of the hunting party, galloped on ahead to Winchester, seized the Royal Treasure deposited there, and on 5 August had himself crowned at Westminster Abbey by the Bishop of London.

The four Norman kings, depicted by Matthew Paris, c.1250. Top left, William I; top right, William II; bottom left, Henry I; bottom right, Stephen. Royal MS 14, Ch. vii, f. 8 v. BRITISH LIBRARY

William II. Wax seal. BRITISH LIBRARY

HENRY I
Born 1068, reigned 1100–1135

STEPHEN
Born c.1097, reigned 1135–1154

When Henry faced accusations that he had illegally usurped the Crown while his elder brother Robert – designated by William Rufus as his heir – was alive, he replied simply that his claim as a son born 'in the purple', that is, while William I was king, was superior to the claims of Robert, and of William Rufus, both born while their father was merely Duke of Normandy. Henry bolstered up this somewhat shaky claim, and pacified his barons by abolishing some of his brother's abuses, marrying Matilda, daughter of the King of Scotland and descendant of the old English line, coming to an agreement with Louis of France and reconciling the Crown to a Church strongly antagonised by William II's blasphemous behaviour. By 1102 England was quiescent. He defeated Robert on his return from the Crusade at the Battle of Tinchebrai in 1106, imprisoned him for life and thereafter ruled a united Normandy and England as the Conqueror had done.

Henry displayed his father's administrative ability, restructuring the Treasury and the Exchequer, and sending travelling justices round the shires, thus laying the foundation for today's Crown Courts. The *Anglo-Saxon Chronicle* nostalgically described the 'lion of justice', as Henry was called during the anarchy of his successor's reign, as: 'a good man . . . held in great awe. In his days no man dared to wrong another. He made peace for man and beast'.

Henry's dynastic ambitions foundered when his only legitimate son and heir, William, was shipwrecked and drowned in 1120. Attempts to induce his barons to accept as ruler his daughter Matilda, widow of the Emperor Henry V, were only partially successful after Henry forced Matilda into a second marriage with the unpopular Geoffrey, Count of Anjou – Anjou was the traditional enemy of Normandy. In the event, when Henry died in 1135 it was his favourite nephew Stephen, son of Henry's sister Adela and the Count of Blois, who assumed the Crown of England.

RIGHT *Henry I. Silver penny, minted in London by the moneyer Wulfgar, c.1108–10.* BRITISH MUSEUM

The speed of Stephen's assumption of the Crown almost equalled that of his uncles, William Rufus in 1087 and Henry I in 1100. His claim, however, was based not on a direct line of inheritance – which would have indicated Henry I's daughter Matilda – but on the notions of 'designation' and 'suitability', both integral elements of medieval king-making. Just as the Conqueror declared that King Edward the Confessor had 'designated' him as successor, and William Rufus declared himself the Conqueror's dying choice, so Stephen, persuading the Archbishop of Canterbury that he had Henry I's dying vote, had himself crowned within three weeks of his uncle's death. When, rather late in the day, Stephen's claim was solemnly debated in 1139, it was upheld by the Pope.

The element of 'suitability' eliminated Matilda on the grounds that the barons had not sworn allegiance to her second husband, Geoffrey of Anjou, that her son and heir (the future Henry II) was only two years old and that in any case at Henry I's death Normandy was at war with Anjou. But Stephen's 'suitability', based on his close acquaintance with the Anglo-Norman barons amongst whom he had been brought up, was to prove illusory. He was unable to control his barons, and the arrival in 1139 of Matilda with her supporters from Anjou – the Angevins – heralded some six years of anarchy in England. 'Never did a country endure greater misery', moaned the Peterborough chronicler in the *Anglo-Saxon Chronicle*.

King Stephen. Silver penny, minted in Thetford by the moneyer Odde, c.1140. BRITISH MUSEUM

Stephen's fortunes ebbed and flowed. He was taken prisoner by Matilda at Lincoln in 1141, but soon rescued by his queen. The latter's supporters captured Matilda's half-brother, Robert of Gloucester, who was directing her campaign, and the two captives were exchanged. Matilda finally departed for Normandy, which her husband had conquered, relinquishing her claim to the English throne to her son Henry, now a dashing youth who mounted two rapid attacks against Stephen in 1147 and 1149. On the death of his father in 1151 Henry, already at nineteen a seasoned soldier and Duke of Normandy, became Count of Anjou and leader of the Angevin faction. His marriage in the same year to the former Queen of France, Eleanor, Duchess of Aquitaine, increased his vast French possessions.

Stephen's attempts to have his elder son, Eustace, crowned during his own lifetime (a practice common in Europe) were frustrated by the Pope's refusal to allow the Archbishop of Canterbury to perform the ceremony. Eustace's sudden death, the arrival of the popular Henry in England and the growing strength of the Angevin party all forced Stephen into a widely-approved compromise: 'the King should be lord and king while he lived and after his day Henry should be king. He was to regard the King as father, and the King him as son, and peace and concord should exist between them and throughout all England . . . Soon there was a good and lasting peace such as had never been here before . . .'. Stephen's death in 1154 paved the way for the arrival of a new dynasty, the Angevins or Plantagenets, on the throne of England.

HENRY II
Born 1133, reigned 1154–1189

The name Plantagenet has its origin in the Count of Anjou's emblem, which was the flower of the broom plant – *plante genêt* in French. Henry II, the first Plantagenet king on the throne of England, had been named after his grandfather, Henry I. The latter's strong government, still fresh in men's memories, was admired and copied by his grandson. Henry's efforts brought England from the anarchy of Stephen's reign back to settled government, and the Exchequer, local government and the royal courts regained their former efficiency.

But when Henry appointed his chancellor and friend, Thomas à Becket, to the key post of Archbishop of Canterbury in 1162, relations between Crown and Church became strained. Becket's swift transition from the role of efficient, loyal, moral yet worldly servant to that of the ascetic man of God (he wrote to Henry: 'You are my lord, you are my king, you are my spiritual son') dismayed and angered the king. A protracted wrangle in the disputed area of the jurisdiction of Church and State, especially in the procedure for dealing with erring clergy, in which Henry attempted to reaffirm ancient royal privileges and Becket to uphold Church law, resulted in Becket's flight to the Pope. In 1170, on his return he was murdered in his own Cathedral of Canterbury by four of Henry's knights, an event which profoundly shocked contemporary society.

Public opinion was appeased by Henry's immediate disclaimer of responsibility and by his dramatic acts of repentance – he walked barefoot through the streets of Canterbury and submitted to a public flogging by several bishops and the Canterbury monks – and also by the Pope's canonisation of the martyred Becket.

Henry was the first English king since 1066 to be fully literate; he liked to have learned men about him and was a generous patron. His interest in legal matters earned him the title 'father of the common law', and the changes and clarifications which he introduced in this field, namely the increased use of the twelve-man jury and the *novel disseisin* writ for use in cases of disputed ownership of land, were important contributions to the development of the English legal system.

For Henry, however, England was only a small part of his huge empire which stretched from the Scottish border almost to the Pyrenees and included more than half of present-day France. His energetic efforts to control not only this vast area but also his quarrelsome family had unhappy results. His eldest son, Henry ('The Young King') whose coronation as King of England his father had arranged in 1170 in an attempt to secure dynastic continuity, engaged in rebellion, as did his other sons, Richard, John and Geoffrey, and his wife Eleanor. 'The Young King' and Geoffrey predeceased their father and Richard allied himself with Philip II of France, his father's enemy. In the ensuing fighting Henry II fell ill and was carried to his castle at Chinon, where he died on 6 July 1189, and was buried in nearby Fontevrault Abbey. His reign, which had begun in triumph, ended in sadness and defeat.

RICHARD I
Born 1157, reigned 1189–1199

Richard was thirty-two years old when he succeeded his father as the second Plantagenet king on the throne of England, and most of his adult life had been spent living, and fighting, on the Continent. Richard, in fact, could not speak English, had little interest in England except as a source of revenue, and during the ten years of his reign visited his kingdom only twice, once for three and later for two months.

Yet paradoxically enough, this king, who felt it was his mission to settle the affairs of every kingdom in Europe and in the Near East while neglecting his own, became an English legend and folk hero under the popular name of 'Richard the Lionheart'. Immediately after his coronation Richard joined the Third Crusade; Jerusalem had fallen to the Saracens under Saladin in 1187 and all Christendom united to win it back. On his way Richard settled the affairs of Sicily, conquered Cyprus and married Berengaria, Princess of Navarre, who was crowned Queen of England. He finally reached Acre in 1191 and assisted in the siege. By October 1192,

having failed to reach the Holy City, he made peace with Saladin and set off home, only to be captured by his old enemy Leopold of Austria and handed over to the Emperor Henry VI who demanded an enormous ransom. When this was eventually paid early in 1194, Richard returned to England, stayed for two months and left for France where he remained until his death.

The fearless 'Lionheart' died, not in the heat of a great battle, but by a shot from a lone crossbowman at the Castle of Chalus-Chabrol held by a handful of supporters of the rebellious Viscount of Limoges. The bolt entered Richard's shoulder and on its removal the wound turned fatally gangrenous. The disposal of Richard's body illustrates the anxiety of medieval churchmen to gain the honour and prestige of providing resting places for royal remains – Richard's entrails were buried in Charroux in Poitou, his heart in Rouen Cathedral and the rest of his body in Fontevrault Abbey beside that of his father Henry II. Richard's Queen, Berengaria, lived on in Le Mans until she died in 1230 and

was buried in nearby L'Epau Abbey. She and Richard had no children, and the Crown of England passed to Richard's brother John.

HIC·COR·CONDITVM·EST·RICARDI
ANGLORVM·REGIS·QVI·COR·LEONIS·DICTVS
OBIIT·AN·M·C·XC·IX

JOHN

Born 1167, reigned 1199–1216

As the fourth son of Henry II and Eleanor, John could not have expected to succeed to his father's throne, and his early life, spent in constant intrigue and fighting against his father and brothers, did little to prepare him for kingship. John's claim, contested by his nephew Arthur of Brittany (son of John's elder brother Geoffrey) was upheld by the Archbishop of Canterbury and William the Marshal, doyen of the Anglo-Norman barons. He was duly crowned at Westminster and entered upon a stormy reign dominated by three areas of dispute.

The first concerned the loss by John, through maladroit intrigues and ineffectual fighting, of almost all the vast Plantagenet dominions in France to the French King Philip. In the second dispute John became embroiled with the Pope in a violent disagreement over the election of a new archbishop of Canterbury which culminated in 1206 with the Pope laying England under edict and excommunicating John. For seven years all the churches were closed, no masses sung, no marriage or funeral services conducted, until in 1213 John surrendered and accepted the Pope's candidate Stephen Langton.

The third dispute, a revolt of the English barons, produced an event with far-reaching consequences for the history of England, the sealing of the Magna Carta by the king. During the reign of Richard, 'the absentee king', some of the machinery of government, notably the Chancery and the Exchequer, had become semi-independent. John's misrule, and his loss of French territory, aggravated the barons' grievances. Casting around for a precedent, they found that at his coronation Henry I had issued a charter listing abuses he promised to rectify. The Chancery department then proceeded, with consultations between John and his barons and the prestigious Stephen Langton and William the Marshal, to draw up such a list of abuses and their remedies. The resulting Magna Carta, to which John set his seal at Runnymede Meadow in June 1215, was based on the assumption that there should exist a recognisable body of law, known to all, to regulate all necessary operations of royal government and relations between king and subject. Magna Carta, originally instigated to redress the grievances of the baronial class, eventually contained so many clauses protecting other interests and privileges, especially of freemen, that it has come to stand as the foundation of English liberty.

John's unhappy reign came to an abrupt end in the following year. He persuaded the Pope to condemn the Magna Carta, the barons responded by attempting to depose him and offer the Crown of England to the Dauphin Louis, son of King Philip of France. In the fighting which followed John lost his baggage-train, which contained his valuable holy relics, in a quicksand at the head of the Wash, succumbed to sickness and died in October 1216, 'released from much bitterness of mind and a life of many disturbances and vain labours', as the chronicler Matthew Paris noted later. John was buried in Worcester Cathedral, and the reign of his nine-year-old son, Henry III, began.

ABOVE
King John's seal on the Magna Carta.
BRITISH LIBRARY

LEFT
Tomb-effigy of King John supported by two bishops, in Worcester Cathedral.
COURTAULD INSTITUTE

13

HENRY III
Born 1207, reigned 1216–1272

It is surprising that a child of nine should be made king with little opposition at a time when a rival claimant, the Dauphin of France, was already in England with his supporters. But a number of factors contributed to place Henry III on the throne. As a young child Henry had made no enemies, the Pope constituted himself as guardian, on the whole the barons preferred a child whom they could influence to the already strong and experienced heir to the French throne and, above all, Henry's claim was supported by the much-respected William the Marshal. His ringing words embody both the high ideals of chivalry, and a determination to adhere to the hereditary 'line of descent': 'By God's sword, if all abandoned the King, do you know what I should do? I would carry him on my shoulders step by step, from island to island, from country to country, and I would not fail him even if it meant begging my bread'.

Under the skilful regency of William until his death in 1219, and then with the support of Archbishop Stephen Langton and the Justiciar (holder of the highest judiciary post) Hubert de Burgh, the early years of the reign passed calmly until Henry came of age in 1227 and his personal rule began. This promising start did not continue. Henry's long reign de- generated into a conflict between his abso-lutist tendencies, and the determination of the barons to exert some measure of control over the Crown, the choice of ministers and the king himself. Although the Magna Carta was reissued several times, this did not suffice. Matters came to a head in 1258 when Henry formally surrendered England's rights in Norman-dy, Anjou and Poitou to the French king, thus effectively marking the end of the Plantagenet Empire, and also surrendered to his baronial opposition with the Provi-sions of Oxford. The latter proposed a new type of government in the form of a Council of Fifteen which had to be con-sulted by the king and which would appoint the justiciar, chancellor and treasurer.

During the next seven years uneasy relations turned into strife and civil war. Simon de Montfort, Earl of Leicester, Henry's brother-in-law, a leading figure in the Provisions and one-time ally of Hen-ry's heir, the Lord Edward, defeated Hen-ry in battle and took him prisoner, holding Edward, who by that time was reconciled with his father and leading his army, hostage. For a year (1264–5), Simon effectively ruled England with the Great Council which significantly, in 1265, cal-led not only upon barons but also upon knights representing the shires and burgesses representing the towns, to attend.

Simon was killed in battle in August 1265, Henry was restored and the last seven years of the reign were relatively peaceful. But Simon's ideas were not forgotten – the notion of ongoing discus-sions between the king and all ruling interests, the 'community of the realm', had been implanted in men's minds and in the still far-off future these 'parleyings' would become England's Parliament. Henry III died in 1272, while Lord Ed-ward was on crusade. Henry, artistic and devout, had for much of his reign been rebuilding and enlarging King Edward the Confessor's Westminster Abbey, and there he was laid to rest.

Tomb-effigy of Henry III in Westminster Abbey. WARBURG INSTITUTE

EDWARD I

Born 1239, reigned 1272–1307

Henry III's son, Lord Edward, was taking part in the Seventh Crusade when his father died. The journey home took him two years, but this confident monarch had no fears for his throne, having been proclaimed king by hereditary right and the barons' will as soon as Henry died.

Edward had proved himself as a soldier during the civil wars of his father's reign and in the Crusade; as King, defied by the Welsh Prince Llewelyn in 1282, he won a total victory. He enforced his authority in Wales by building strategically placed castles at Conway, Caernarvon, Beaumaris and Harlech, and in 1301 he bestowed on his son, the future Edward II, the title of Prince of Wales, a title held to this day by the eldest son of the monarch. It was during this campaign that Edward started to train his infantry in the use of the longbow, a weapon he borrowed from the Welsh and which would prove its worth during the reign of his grandson, Edward III, at the battles of Crécy and Poitiers. Such was the force of the longbow that the arrow it despatched was said to be capable of pinning the thigh of a rider in full armour, through his saddle, to his horse's side.

The real achievements of Edward's reign, however, were in the fields of law and government. Nicknamed 'the English Justinian' after the Emperor who codified Roman law, Edward embarked upon an immense programme of legislation, providing, with his statutes, the basis of modern land law. That these statutes were passed through Parliament was one of Edward's innovations, as were his Parliaments themselves. Having closely observed Simon de Montfort's experiments, Edward realised that frequently-held national assemblies could only facilitate government, and that by including among their members local knights from the shires and burgesses from the towns he would have the support of a much broader spectrum of society. His motive was the strengthening of royal power, not the introduction of democracy, but among the unexpected results of his innovations were

the beginnings of the political education of Englishmen – when the knights and burgesses went home from the assemblies and explained the King's policy to their communities – and the first faint stirrings of a sense of national needs and national unity.

Edward's successes did not include a conquest of Scotland. Claiming to be overlord, Edward made several expeditions north. Although the Scottish Coronation Stone of Scone was seized and removed to Westminster Abbey, the Scots under William Wallace and later Robert the Bruce repelled Edward's threat to their independence.

In 1254 Edward, at fifteen, had married Eleanor, daughter of the King of Castile. When she died in 1290 in Nottingham, Edward's grief prompted him to erect crosses at each place where her body rested on its way to burial in Westminster Abbey, the last one being Charing Cross in London. In 1298 he married his second wife Margaret, daughter of King Philip of France. Edward died in 1307 while marching north against the Scots. His body was brought home in slow procession to Westminster, and the tragic reign of his son, Edward II, began.

EDWARD II
Born 1284, reigned 1307–1327

EDWARD III
Born 1312, reigned 1327–1377

The French chronicler Jean Froissart, writing some forty years after the death of Edward II, sagely observed: 'The English will never love or honour their sovereign unless he be victorious and a lover of arms'. Edward II's tragedy began with his failure as a military leader. His half-hearted attempts to subdue Scotland whose leader, Robert the Bruce, had been crowned King Robert I in 1306, culminated in the crushing defeat of the English army at Bannockburn in 1314. For the remainder of Edward's reign King Robert could send his raiding parties over the border into England with impunity.

Edward was no more successful at governing and, unlike his father, Edward I, he had no head for business. His lax rule, neglect of royal duties and infatuation for his favourite, the Gascon Piers Gaveston, forced his barons, in 1310, to impose upon him a set of reforming Ordinances drawn up by Parliament, thus bringing about virtual rule by these Lords Ordainers. The capture and murder of Gaveston by the barons in 1312 resulted in a prolonged period of strife and misrule. Edward acquired two new favourites, the Despensers father and son, both named Hugh, the father being a Lord of the Welsh Marches, and with their help overcame his enemies at the Battle of Boroughbridge in 1322. The Ordinances were then repealed and royal authority reasserted for the time being.

Edward had married Isabella, daughter of King Philip of France, in 1308, and she had borne him four children. In 1325 she was sent, together with her eldest son Edward, then aged thirteen (the future Edward III) on a diplomatic mission to France. There she met Roger Mortimer, one of the disaffected Marcher lords exiled after the Battle of Boroughbridge. Isabella and Mortimer became lovers and planned a rebellion. By betrothing young Prince Edward to Philippa, the eleven-year-old daughter of the Count of Hainault, they were able to use her dowry to obtain men and arms and in 1326 they invaded England, meeting little resistance. The Despensers were hunted down and killed, Edward II was abandoned by his few supporters and a Parliament was summoned which forced him to abdicate and relinquish the throne to his son. At first the deposed king was confined at Kenilworth Castle. After rebellious disturbances in the Midlands, he was moved to Berkeley Castle in Gloucestershire, met his death there, by means unknown, and was buried in Gloucester Cathedral. Froissart's sad comment: 'they shortened his life for him. So ended that King of England and we shall speak no more of him', draws a veil over the tragedy of Edward II.

That Edward III's fifty years on the throne would turn out to be one of the most brilliant reigns of the House of Plantagenet could never have been foretold when the crown of the deposed Edward II was placed on the head of his fifteen-year-old son in January 1327. The first three years of the young Edward III's reign were stained with shame and dishonour: his imprisoned father was murdered some nine months after the coronation, his mother and Mortimer lived openly together. Their joint rule was ruthless and rapacious and Mortimer steadily assumed kingly powers.

But Edward III developed into a confident man of action. In 1330, aged eighteen, he staged a swift coup – entering Nottingham Castle at night with loyal followers by a secret passage, he arrested Mortimer. Displaying a maturity beyond his years, he refrained from killing him on the spot. Instead, next morning he placed his prisoner in the Tower to await trial, issued a proclamation that he was taking the government into his own hands and sent out writs summoning Parliament. This assembly found Mortimer guilty on a list of charges, including that of murdering Edward II, and he was put to death. As for his mother Isabella, 'the she-wolf of France', Edward settled her in comfortable retirement at Castle Rising in Norfolk.

Edward's mature handling of this crisis set the tone for a reign in which he restored royal prestige, initially with the military successes expected by the country. Winning major victories against the Scots at Dupplin Moor in 1332 and Halidon Hill in 1333, Edward placed his candidate Edward Balliol on the throne of Scotland, only for the English to be driven out again in 1341.

By that time, however, Edward was at war with France. Hostilities started in 1337 in defence of Edward's claim through his mother to the French throne, from which he was excluded by France's adoption of the Salic Law forbidding succession through the female line. And so the Hundred Years War

Alabaster tomb-effigy of Edward II in Gloucester Cathedral. WOODMANSTERNE

began. An early English success in the war was Edward's victory in the sea battle of Sluys in 1340. Edward was proclaimed 'Lord of the Sea' and a gold coin was struck portraying him armed and crowned in a ship. Land victories followed: in 1346 at Crécy where his eldest son Edward, the Black Prince, aged sixteen, gave proof of his brilliance as a commander. (When the future King Edward VIII visited the battlefield of Crécy during the First World War in 1917, he was surprised to learn that he was the first Prince of Wales to set foot on that historic field since the Black Prince). The battle of Poitiers in 1356 was as brilliant a success as Crécy, largely due to the tactical superiority of the English longbowmen, skilled in the use of that deadly weapon first introduced by Edward I. Calais was taken, after a long siege, in 1347 – and if the story of Edward yielding to Queen Philippa's pleas to spare the lives of its governor and leading burghers who were courageously marching out to give themselves up with ropes already round their necks is no more than a legend, it would be in keeping with Edward's sense of kingly dignity, Philippa's compassionate nature and the affectionate relationship of the royal couple. That these amiable characteristics were known to a later royal couple was pleasantly demonstrated when, in 1842, Queen Victoria and Prince Albert gave a fancy dress ball and chose to go as their ancestors, Queen Philippa and Edward III. Victoria, delighted with their costumes, made 'rough sketches' of them in her journal, and then commissioned Landseer to commemorate the event in a painting; visiting Westminster Abbey with Albert after the ball to view the

RICHARD II
Born 1367, reigned 1377–1399

tomb-effigies of Philippa and Edward, she expressed disappointment that Philippa's effigy was so badly worn.

Edward III did not share the interest of his grandfather, Edward I, in law-making, preferring to involve Parliament in his military activities, thus strengthening its power to supply, or refuse, war funds. A growing sense of national unity was encouraged when English was made the official language of the law courts in 1362, and when Parliament was opened in 1363 by a chancellor speaking, for the first time, in English. Edward held brilliant court, creating the knightly Order of the Garter, sponsoring writers including his page Geoffrey Chaucer, and exercising artistic patronage. The now-demolished wall-paintings in St Stephen's Chapel in Westminster of himself, Philippa and their large family of twelve children displayed Edward's interest not so much in 'royal faces' as in genealogy.

Edward's last years were clouded by the death of Philippa in 1369, and of the Black Prince from dropsy in 1376, by the political manoeuvres of his fourth son John of Gaunt and by military reverses in which England had to give up all of her territories in France except for the district round Calais. Edward died in 1377 and was laid to rest in Westminster Abbey. His successor on the throne of England was the Black Prince's ten-year-old son, Richard II.

Edward III had 'designated' his grand-son Richard as his heir, and although three of Edward's adult sons were still alive and the dangers of having a child king were apparent to all, his wish to continue the direct line of descent was respected. The ten-year-old Richard was crowned within a month of his grandfather's death and placed under the regency of his uncle, Edward III's fourth son, John of Gaunt, Duke of Lancaster. This powerful and ambitious man never attained the Crown himself, but the son of his first marriage founded the House of Lancaster as Henry IV, and his great-granddaughter by his third marriage – Margaret Beaufort – was the mother of Henry VII, founder of the House of Tudor.

When Richard II was fourteen he bravely faced the angry mob of the Peasants' Revolt led by Wat Tyler. But the young king's promises to redress their grievances were never fulfilled – an

unhappy beginning to a stormy reign. Richard's struggles to dominate his barons and assert the royal prerogative were at first ineffectual, but by 1389 he had regained power, set up his private army wearing his emblem of a white hart and executed or exiled his opponents, among them his cousin Henry of Bolingbroke, the eldest son of John of Gaunt, whom he banished to France for six years in 1398.

When John of Gaunt died in 1399, Richard extended Henry's banishment for life and seized the rich Lancaster estates. This action brought to a head the discontent occasioned by Richard's increasing despotism. Henry returned from France, collected an army, seized Richard and induced him to abdicate. Parliament was summoned and shown the empty throne. The charges against Richard, including the accusation that he had broken his coronation oath by ruling according to his own pleasure rather than by law, were read out. Henry, claiming the Crown by descent, rightful conquest and the necessity of saving the realm, ascended the throne as Henry IV. Richard was moved from the Tower of London to Henry's Pontefract Castle.

An abortive revolt by some of his

Tomb-effigy of Edward III in Westminster Abbey.

Richard II. Panel portrait, c.1395, in Westminster Abbey.

The Wilton Diptych: Richard II is presented by John the Baptist, St Edmund and King Edward the Confessor (left wing) to the Virgin and angels (right wing). NATIONAL GALLERY

HENRY IV
Born 1367, reigned 1399–1413

When Henry of Bolingbroke, so named after the Lincolnshire village in which he was born, forced his cousin Richard II to abdicate and set himself on the throne as the first member of the House of Lancaster, he was thirty-two years old. His life until then had been spent in fighting all over Europe, and in exile in France. His fourteen-year reign was a troubled one, as his rule did not go unchallenged.

Revolts broke out among the Welsh under their national leader Owen Glendower, the powerful Percy family from Northumberland under Lord Henry 'Hotspur' Percy rebelled, and the Scots under the Earl of Douglas invaded English territory. With the help of his young son, the future Henry V, the king won a resounding victory at Shrewsbury in 1403 when Hotspur was killed, Douglas was taken prisoner and the enemy routed. By 1409 Glendower had ceased to be a menace.

In France the struggle between the Armagnacs and the Burgundians to gain control of the mad King Charles VI resulted in both sides turning to Henry IV for help. Some small expeditions were sent across the Channel, forerunners of the successful campaigns of the next reign. Henry IV's domestic troubles centred on the growing Lollard movement advocating Church reform, and on his powerful barons struggling to control his Council. When he died, ill and worn out, in 1413, these problems remained to confront his son who came to the throne as Henry V.

of Anne of Bohemia, his first wife who had died in 1394, in the tomb Richard had prepared for them both where their tomb effigies lay holding hands.

Richard's extravagance – one of the charges levelled against him – may have contributed to his downfall, but in the field of artistic patronage he bequeathed to posterity not only his extensive rebuilding at Westminster Abbey and the magnificent hammer-beam, angel-adorned roof of Westminster Hall, but two splendidly enigmatic portraits of himself: it has been suggested that the panel painting in Westminster Abbey showing the young king in coronation robes may have been intended to sit as a permanent effigy in the king's stall in the choir; the Wilton Diptych, now in London's National Gallery, depicts him as an ardent donor, protected by John the Baptist, St Edmund and King Edward the Confessor, adoring a Virgin and Child whose massed ranks of angels carry on their breasts Richard's white hart emblem – underlining the conflicting qualities of humble devotion and regal arrogance of the last king of the House of Plantagenet.

supporters in January 1400 sealed Richard's fate, and he died, by means unknown, at Pontefract two weeks later. Eager to convince the populace that there had been no foul play, Henry IV had Richard's body, face uncovered, carried in slow procession through the countryside to the royal residence at King's Langley for burial. Not until 1413, in a gracious gesture of atonement by King Henry V, was his body removed to Westminster Abbey to lie beside that

Electrotypes of the tomb-effigies of Richard II and Anne of Bohemia in Westminster Abbey. NATIONAL PORTRAIT GALLERY

Tomb-effigies of Henry IV and Joan of Navarre in Trinity Chapel, Canterbury Cathedral. WOODMANSTERNE

HENRY V
Born 1387, reigned 1413–1422

Henry V was twenty-five years old when he came to the throne on a wave of popularity. He had been a soldier since childhood – at the age of twelve he was knighted by Richard II in the field during the Irish campaign of 1399, when sixteen he fought alongside his father at the Battle of Shrewsbury and then, as Prince of Wales he was given sole responsibility to carry on the war against Owen Glendower.

That England saw Henry primarily as a warrior king is apparent from the petition presented by Parliament in 1414 which referred to his 'adversary of France'. The preparations to send Henry's expeditionary force across the Channel in 1415 mark him out as an expert administrator, and his celebrated victory at Agincourt shows him to have been an experienced general and inspired leader of men. Henry and his army received an ecstatic welcome when they returned laden with spoils and an impressive array of noble prisoners. Two years later he mounted his second, and larger, invasion of France. This campaign ended triumphantly in 1420 with the Treaty of Troyes by which Henry married Catherine of Valois, daughter of

Henry V, aged twelve, being knighted by Richard II in the field. Harley MS 1319, f. 5. BRITISH LIBRARY

Charles VI, was recognised as regent and was to be King of France on Charles' death. This astonishing success was enthusiastically celebrated when Henry and Catherine arrived in England in January 1421 and embarked on a triumphal tour of the kingdom. In June Henry set off again for France and in December, while he was besieging Meaux, news reached him of the birth of his son, the future Henry VI.

Henry V's life came to an abrupt end at Vincennes in August 1422. England's 'hero-king' faced death, from an unidentifiable disease, as calmly as he had faced overwhelming odds at Agincourt, and made careful arrangements for the regency of his infant son. His impressive funeral procession took three months to reach London. At the magnificent ceremony in Westminster Abbey his stricken subjects watched three favourite warhorses of their 'king of kings' being led solemnly to the high altar. Sculptures in Henry's superb chantry chapel show him on his throne, and at full gallop on his charger. Henry's widow Catherine, mother of the last member of the House

of Lancaster on the throne, became, by her marriage to Owen Tudor, grandmother of Henry VII, first of the House of Tudor.

Henry V. Panel painting, artist unknown.
NATIONAL PORTRAIT GALLERY

Funeral effigy of Henry V's Queen, Catherine of Valois Undercroft Museum.
THE DEAN AND CHAPTER OF WESTMINSTER

HENRY VI
Born 1421, reigned 1422–1461

EDWARD IV
Born 1441, reigned 1461–1483

Henry VI inherited none of his father's war-like qualities. He was gentle, devout and scholarly, and suffered, like his grandfather Charles VI of France, from bouts of madness. From the regency of his uncles in his early years Henry fell in 1445 under the domination of his wife, Margaret of Anjou, and the manipulation of his nobles.

The state of England, already unstable at the end of Henry V's reign, worsened. The king's weak rule and the quarrelling between factions led inevitably to civil war. Henry IV's usurping of the throne proved fatal for his grandson when Richard, Duke of York, declared his claim, through Edward III's second son, to be superior to that of the King. The ensuing Wars of the Roses between the Houses of Lancaster and York subjected the country to some thirty years of bloody conflict, lawlessness and disorder. Henry VI was defeated in battle in 1461 and deposed by Edward, son of the then dead Richard of York, who seized the Crown as Edward IV. Henry, by then permanently insane, was imprisoned. He was briefly reinstated, as a puppet king, in 1470 by the powerful Earl of Warwick, the 'king-maker', but in 1471 was captured and put to death by Edward IV.

Edward IV was nineteen years old when, with the help of his kinsman the 'king-maker' Earl of Warwick, he seized the Crown in 1461. The first ten years of Edward's reign were a period of bitter strife between the Houses of York and Lancaster. In 1470 the 'king-maker' changed sides, placed the deranged Henry VI on the throne and virtually governed the country himself for a year. Edward fled to the Continent to seek help and his suffering countrymen waited for the outcome – 'the world is right queasy', one anxious onlooker wrote.

1471 saw Edward's triumphant re-seizure of the Crown with Burgundian aid. The subsequent deaths of Henry VI

Edward IV. Panel painting, c.1532–40, unknown artist, perhaps commissioned by King Henry VIII.
ROYAL COLLECTION

Henry VI. Panel painting, unknown artist.
NATIONAL PORTRAIT GALLERY

EDWARD V

Born 1470, reigned April–June 1483

and his only son signalled the end of the House of Lancaster and the rise of the House of York. In 1461 Edward IV owed his Crown to the Earl of Warwick; but in 1471 he resumed it with an enhanced reputation, regaining it through his own resourcefulness, determination and brilliant military skill.

Edward's Treaty of Picquigny with King Louis of France brought him a pension which made him independent of Parliamentary grants for the rest of his reign and gave England increased trade, thus pleasing the powerful London merchants favoured by the king. Financially secure, Edward ran a splendid court with his queen, Elizabeth Woodville, patronised artists and writers and encouraged building, his architectural masterpiece being St George's Chapel at Windsor Castle. When in 1483 Edward died unexpectedly at the age of 42 – as the Croyland Chronicler noted: 'neither worn out with old age nor yet seized with any known kind of malady' – his foreign policy of playing off France and Burgundy against each other lay in ruins when these traditional enemies agreed to the Treaty of Arras and thus made peace. Edward was laid to rest in his still unfinished Chapel at Windsor, bequeathing a troubled inheritance to his twelve-year-old son, Edward V.

When Edward IV died on 9 April 1483 his young son, Edward, was in Wales where he had been established with his own household since 1475. He and his governor, his maternal uncle Earl Rivers, immediately set off for London. On the way they met Richard, Earl of Gloucester, brother of Edward IV, who had been appointed by the dying King as Protector of the Realm. Richard entered London with his nephew, and the boy was proclaimed as King Edward V and Richard confirmed as Protector.

In June Parliament declared Edward IV's marriage to Elizabeth Woodville to have been bigamous because of his supposed pre-contract to another lady. All his children were declared illegitimate, the young King Edward V and his brother Prince Richard were put in the Tower of London and their uncle ascended the throne as Richard III. The 'Princes in the Tower' were never seen alive again. What were presumed to be

The uncrowned Edward V. Panel of Kings, St George's Chapel, Windsor Castle.
THE DEAN AND CANONS OF WINDSOR

their bones, found at the foot of a staircase in the Tower of London, lie quietly now in a little sarcophagus in Westminster Abbey, placed there by the order of King Charles II in 1674.

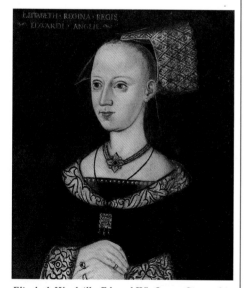

Elizabeth Woodville, Edward IV's Queen. Sixteenth-century copy of a panel painting, unknown artist.
ASHMOLEAN MUSEUM

Edward V (when Prince of Wales) stands beside his father, Edward IV, and his mother, to receive a presentation volume of an English translation (c.1477) of Les Dictes des Philosophes *from the translator, Earl Rivers (the prince's governor). MS 265.* LAMBETH PALACE LIBRARY

RICHARD III
Born 1452, reigned 1483–1485

Eleven years younger than Edward IV, Richard, Earl of Gloucester, spent his youth in his brother's service, loyally supporting him through the turmoil of the Wars of the Roses, accompanying him on his flight to the Continent and sharing in his triumphant return in 1471. An able soldier and experienced administrator, Richard was sent to uphold the king's authority in the north and succeeded in reconciling that turbulent area to the House of York. When, in 1483, Edward IV realised that he was dying, he appointed Richard as Protector, having no reason to doubt his loyalty. Edward, however, had not taken into account the hostility between his brother and his queen. His marriage to Elizabeth Woodville and the subsequent enriching and advancement of her many relatives had aroused jealousy and fear, as had the appointment of the queen's brother as governor to the heir. The general fear that a long minority and quarrels between Protector Richard and the queen's relatives would result in weak government and possibly renewed civil war, enabled Richard to proclaim himself king and rid himself of some of the queen's party without much opposition from a country which largely trusted him and approved of his past loyalty to his brother.

But the disappearance of the two sons of the popular Edward IV, the little 'Princes in the Tower', aroused a strong feeling of revulsion against Richard which could not be quelled and which fragmented the Yorkist party. Rebellions broke out and his followers fell away. When Henry Tudor, claimant to the throne, landed in Milford Haven in August 1485, supporters rallied to his standard. Richard, the last Yorkist king, was killed at the Battle of Bosworth, and Henry Tudor ascended the throne as Henry VII, the first monarch of the House of Tudor.

RICARDVS · III · ANG · REX ·

Richard III. Sixteenth-century copy of a panel painting, unknown artist.
NATIONAL PORTRAIT GALLERY

HENRY VII

Born 1457, reigned 1485–1509

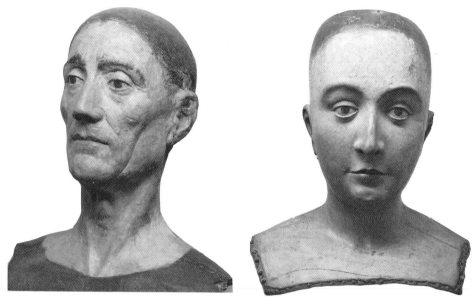

The funeral effigies of Henry VII and Elizabeth of York. Undercroft Museum.
THE DEAN AND CHAPTER OF WESTMINSTER

Henry VII was twenty-eight years old when he came to the throne and his relatively peaceful twenty-four-year reign was a remarkable contrast to the turbulent years which had led up to it. Henry was the grandson of Queen Catherine of Valois, daughter of King Charles VI of France and widow of Henry V. Catherine's second marriage, to Owen Tudor, a gentleman of her court, brought forth a son, Edmund Tudor, Earl of Richmond. In 1456 Edmund married the thirteen-year-old Margaret Beaufort – learned daughter of the Duke of Somerset who traced his ancestry back to Edward III – and their son Henry was born in the following year. Henry's claims to the throne of England, therefore, on both his mother's and his father's side, although rather obscure and convoluted, were powerful enough to be a danger to any reigning monarch through the troubled days of mid-fifteenth-century England.

Henry spent most of his youth as a refugee at European courts, in particular in Brittany where Duke Francis used him as a pawn in the complicated political games he played with Edward IV. Henry's abortive invasion against Richard III in November 1483 led to his retreat to France, his successful invasion from there with French help in August 1485 and his victory at the Battle of Bosworth where the crown of England was snatched from the dead Richard III and placed on his brow.

While still a refugee in Brittany Henry had sworn a solemn oath on Christmas Day 1483 that when he became King of England he would bring peace to the warring Houses of York and Lancaster by marrying Elizabeth of York, eldest daughter of Edward IV (a move which would also, by continuing Edward IV's line, stifle possible protests against Henry's assumption of the Crown). Henry married Elizabeth on 18 January 1486, and she bore him four children: Arthur (who died of consumption in 1502), Henry (the future Henry VIII), Margaret and Mary. Elizabeth died in childbirth in 1503, aged thirty-seven, and her funeral effigy was taken in procession to Westminster Abbey on a sumptuously-decorated hearse through crowds mourning her as the daughter of the still-remembered and loved Edward IV.

Henry VII, who had seized the Crown by force with foreign help, pursued a dual aim throughout his reign: to make his kingdom stable, united, independent and financially solvent, and to establish his dynasty, beyond all doubt, upon the throne. To achieve the first he promoted trade with Denmark, Florence, France and the Low Countries, encouraged English shipping with his Navigation Acts of 1485 and 1490, restored law and order to a country sick of civil war by, among other means, the Court of the Star Chamber in which the King's Council sat in a judicial capacity, reorganised the taxation system, introduced economies into all government organisations and struck a firm balance between Church and State by carefully obtaining Church approval and support while maintaining the rights of the Crown. As for his dynastic aim, he ruthlessly put down the many attempts by potential claimants to seize the throne – no mean feat without a standing army – and gradually strengthened his position with diplomatic marriages. His eldest son Arthur was wed to Catherine of Aragon, daughter of King Ferdinand of Spain, in 1501, and his daughter Margaret to King James IV of Scotland in 1503.

Henry's dynastic preoccupations did not recognise the element of portraiture – the popularisation of the 'royal face' was still to come in the reign of his son, Henry VIII. Portraits were still vague, stylised and relying heavily on accessories to identify the sitter. Only the little panel by 'Master Michiel' (Michiel Sittow), painted when a marriage was mooted between the widowed Henry and Margaret of Austria, gives a tantalising glimpse of the enigmatic King. But it is, strangely enough, the plaster funeral effigy, taken from Henry's death-mask, which offers, in death, the most impressive, striking, realistic and 'living' image of a man who was in life the most inscrutable of monarchs.

The gallant young adventurer who had rallied his supporters on Bosworth Field with martial cries had, by the end of his reign, become 'England's policeman', restoring law and order to a country sadly in need of stability. Changes were taking place in the social order; the revival of trade brought to the fore a new class of men whose loyalty to the Crown, to which they owed everything, was unquestioned and who provided a counterbalance to the old nobility. Henry's son, Henry VIII, was able to succeed to a kingdom amid joyful salutations, as Lord Mountjoy wrote to the humanist scholar Erasmus: 'Heaven and earth rejoices; everything is full of milk and honey and nectar', due to the efforts of his father who had securely laid the foundations of the Tudor dynasty.

Henry VII. Panel Painting by Michiel Sittow, 1505. NATIONAL PORTRAIT GALLERY

HENRY VIII
Born 1491, reigned 1509–1547

Although, as a second son, Henry VIII could not have been expected to succeed to his father's throne, he nevertheless received a very thorough education through the influence of his grandmother, the learned Margaret Beaufort, patron of scholars and founder of Christ's and St John's Colleges, Cambridge. Henry acquired knowledge not only of languages – Latin, Greek, French, Italian and Spanish – but also of mathematics and astronomy, as well as developing an interest in matters of theology, which in later years was to spur him on to write his treatise against Luther, the *Assertio Septem Sacramentorum* (*The Defence of the Seven Sacraments*) which was published in 1521. When Erasmus, on a visit to his friend Thomas More in 1499, met the eight-year-old Henry, he was much impressed by the precocious and poised young prince who sent him 'a little note, to challenge something from my pen'. The untimely death in 1502 of Arthur, heir to the throne, focused attention on Henry. When he acceded in April 1509 he was the very ideal of a Renaissance prince, a tall seventeen-year-old, universally acknowledged to be extremely handsome, of splendid physique, a tireless horseman and sportsman, a graceful dancer, a gifted composer and musician able to play the lute, harp, organ and virginals, and a frequenter of scholars. As Erasmus noted: 'There are more men of learning to be found in Henry's Court than in any University'.

Henry's long reign of thirty-seven years brought about immense and lasting changes in his kingdom. In the realm of foreign policy his lasting rivalry with the other two young monarchs of Europe, Francis I of France and the Emperor Charles V, led Cardinal Thomas Wolsey and then the king and his subsequent advisers to perfect a balance-of-power policy. Henry brought his kingdom back into the mainstream of European affairs and at his death England was a force to be reckoned with in Europe.

His break with the Church of Rome, which impressed the Continent, had the

LEFT
Henry VIII (left) and his father Henry VII (right). Preparatory ink and water-colour cartoon for the Whitehall Palace mural by Hans Holbein, 1536–7.
NATIONAL PORTRAIT GALLERY

RIGHT
Henry VIII by Joos van Cleve.
ROYAL COLLECTION

effect at home not only of establishing a national Church of England and giving to his subjects what has been called the unity of being 'entire Englishmen', but also of creating a kingdom which owed allegiance to no outside authority. The Great 'Bible in Englyshe' was printed in 1539 and in 1545 Henry broke the monopoly of Latin-language religious services by allowing the first official English primer, a simple prayer-book in English, to be used. His title of 'Defender of the Faith', previously bestowed upon him by the Pope, has been retained through the long line of monarchs to the

present day. By perfecting the administrative organisation, restructuring central and local government and setting up four new financial courts he and his ministers afforded England much 'good gouvernance'.

Although mainly preoccupied with land war against France, Henry was the first monarch to be deeply and constructively interested in ships; when he visited Southampton in 1518 he had the guns of his galleys 'fired again and again, marking their range', being 'very curious about matters of this kind'. He transformed the English Navy by changing

Catherine of Aragon, first wife of Henry VIII. Panel painting, unknown artist.
NATIONAL PORTRAIT GALLERY

Anne Boleyn, second wife of Henry VIII. Panel painting, unknown artist.
NATIONAL PORTRAIT GALLERY

Jane Seymour, third wife of Henry VIII. Drawing in black and coloured chalks, by Holbein.
WINDSOR CASTLE, ROYAL LIBRARY

the fighting vessel from a floating platform grappling its opponent, to a floating battery of ranks of guns trained to fire the broadside. His daughter, Elizabeth I, when threatened by the might of the Spanish Armada, was to be grateful in this respect to the efforts and foresight of her father, rightly called the 'Father of the English Navy'.

Henry married six times. His first marriage in 1509 following his accession, to Catherine of Aragon, widow of his brother Arthur and daughter of King Ferdinand of Spain, lasted until about 1527. Catherine, her husband's companion in court entertainments, music and dancing, was also his intellectual equal and his trusted consort whom he appointed Governor of the Realm and captain-general of the forces for home defences in 1513 when he went off to war in France. Henry's disappointment at Catherine's failure, after several miscarriages, still-born and short-lived babies, to bear a living son (she produced only one daughter, Mary), his disillusion with both Catherine's father and her nephew the Emperor Charles V as allies and, above all, his infatuation with Anne Boleyn, led to the divorce in 1533 and England's break with the Church of Rome. Catherine died in January 1536. Henry's marriage to Anne Boleyn in 1533 lasted for three years. Producing only a daughter, Elizabeth, Anne was rejected; denounced by the enemies she had made during her rise to power and found guilty of treasonable adultery she perished on the execution block on 19 May 1536. Eleven days later Henry married Jane Seymour, maid-of-honour to both Catherine and Anne. Jane gave birth to the long-awaited heir, the future Edward VI, at Hampton Court on 12 October 1537 and died twelve days later. For the next two years Henry and his ministers sought a diplomatic marriage which would strengthen England against the alliance formed by the French king and the emperor. Their choice fell upon Anne of Cleves, sister of the duke of a Protestant German state. The marriage in January 1540 ended a few months later in an

Anne of Cleves, fourth wife of Henry VIII. Miniature by Holbein, c.1539. VICTORIA & ALBERT MUSEUM

Miniature by Holbein, traditionally considered to depict Catherine Howard, fifth wife of Henry VIII; recent research supports this attribution.
ROYAL COLLECTION

Catherine Parr, sixth wife of Henry VIII. Panel painting, unknown artist.
NATIONAL PORTRAIT GALLERY

amicable divorce whereby Anne was pensioned off, remaining on friendly terms with Henry and residing comfortably in England until her death in 1557. On 28 July 1540 Henry married Catherine Howard, maid-of-honour to Anne of Cleves and young cousin to Anne Boleyn. Two years later, on 13 February 1542, Catherine suffered the same fate as Anne, being bchcadcd on Tower Green on charges of treasonable adultery. Henry's sixth and final marriage to Catherine Parr took place on 12 July 1543. Catherine, aged thirty-one and twice widowed, not only looked after the ageing and ailing Henry but also mothered her three royal step-children, occupying herself with their material as well as their intellectual needs. Patron of enlightened scholars and humanists, her own book of *Prayers Stirring the Mind unto Heavenly Meditations* was printed in 1545 and was soon followed by an enlarged edition. After Henry's death Catherine married Thomas Seymour, brother of Protector Somerset, in 1547 and died in childbirth in 1548.

Henry showed himself fully aware of artistic trends on the Continent by embarking upon an ambitious programme of building, refurbishing existing royal residences, planning new ones (for example the now-demolished Nonesuch Palace which was to have been England's answer to Francis I's Fontainebleau), and even adding touches to other people's houses – when sheltering from plague-stricken London in Cardinal Wolsey's country house at Tittenhanger, he amused himself by having a new window made in Wolsey's closet because the existing one was 'so little'. As for portraiture, Henry soon realised its importance to a Renaissance prince when, in 1526, a gift of miniatures from the French king, Henry's rival not only in the field of politics but also in that of culture, astonished the English court. Stirred to emulation, Henry commissioned the talented Hornebolte family who had recently arrived from the Low Countries and settled in England, to produce for him similar miniatures, or pictures 'in little'. Then in

Hans Holbein the Younger, who arrived in England soon afterwards, Henry found the ideal artist to exploit the potential of the portrait to the full. Holbein's mural painting in the Privy Chamber at Whitehall Palace was commissioned by Henry in 1537 as a visible manifestation of the Tudor dynasty, and

so it appeared to contemporary viewers. But the mural (unhappily destroyed by fire in 1698 and known only from later copies and half of Holbein's original cartoon preserved in the National Portrait Gallery) has also bequeathed to posterity the personal image of Henry with which he will always be associated.

Henry's achievements in bringing England into the Renaissance and Reformation movements and awakening a national consciousness cannot obliterate the dark patches of his reign, the many disappointments, betrayals of friends and reversals of policy. The brilliant young prince who inherited a full exchequer from his father left England in debt, his subjects in a state of religious confusion and his ministers in bitter rivalry. But the monarch of whom it had been said at the beginning of his reign: 'Our King is not after gold, or gems, or precious metals, but virtue, glory, immortality', died peacefully in his bed, happy in having a son to succeed him, and trusting in God. To Archbishop Cranmer, anxiously entreating the speechless king on his death-bed to give him a sign of that trust, Henry responded by 'holding him with his hand, did wring his hand in his as hard as he could', and shortly after passed away.

EDWARD VI

Born 1537, reigned 1547–1553

The death of Henry VIII in 1547 came as a shock to his three children – Mary then aged thirty-one, Elizabeth thirteen and Edward ten – who, under the kind guardianship of Catherine Parr, had become very close. When the news was given to Elizabeth and Edward at Enfield, they clung together and sobbed for the loss of the father whom they had loved. On his deathbed Henry had appointed Jane Seymour's brother, Edward, Duke of Somerset, as Protector. Edward's short reign of six years witnessed a bitter struggle for control of the boy king between Somerset and his rival the Earl of Warwick, which ended in the execution of Somerset and the ascendance of Warwick, whom the young king later created Duke of Northumberland.

Edward was a precocious, intelligent child, educated by eminent scholars and carefully prepared from his nursery days to take his place on the throne. At the age of eight he had been commanded by his father to welcome, on his own, a French state visit led by Claude d'Annebault, Admiral of France. Edward wrote in some anxiety to his stepmother, Catherine Parr, about his speech of greeting: since he had only just started to learn French, did she think that the admiral would understand Latin? In the event his speech was well received, with eager spectators marvelling at his 'high wit and great audacity'. Riding beside the elderly admiral and clasping his hand, the little boy managed his horse perfectly and bore himself with dignity.

Like his father Edward was fond of hunting, tilting, tennis and all outdoor sports; ambassadors seeking an audience sometimes complained that he had 'gone out to play'. From his fourteenth birthday his education ostensibly came

Edward VI. Artist unknown.
NATIONAL PORTRAIT GALLERY

to an end, but Edward, apart from conscientiously performing his administrative duties, pursued all his scholarly interests, and particularly his intense interest in matters of theology. Lasting memorials to Edward's reign are the many schools which bear his name, and the two Prayer Books, issued in 1549 and 1552, to the second of which the young king made many amendments and alterations.

Edward's 'royal face' was depicted at all stages of his short life, from babyhood to the last representations of the frail boy gallantly imitating the stance in which Holbein had immortalised Henry VIII. After increasing periods of ill health Edward succumbed to pulmonary tuber-

culosis on 6 July 1553, lying in the arms of his childhood friend, Henry Sidney, and his Gentleman of the Bedchamber, Thomas Wroth, who supported him between them until he died. 'England's Treasure', as he had been called at his birth, was buried a month later in the Henry VII Chapel of Westminster Abbey beneath the high altar.

The month which passed between the death of Edward VI and his funeral was taken up with events which horrified the grieving population and during which the Crown of England hung in the balance. The dying Edward had been persuaded by the Duke of Northumberland, playing upon the young king's fears of leaving his kingdom in the hands of his Catholic sister Mary, to produce his Device for the Succession. This document removed Mary and Elizabeth from the succession and bestowed the Crown on Lady Jane Grey, the young granddaughter of Henry VIII's sister, Mary. The Duke of Northumberland had previously forced Lady Jane to marry his own son, intending by this means to control the throne. On Edward's death Northumberland immediately proclaimed Jane as queen and rallied his troops, only to be defeated by Mary's supporters who quickly placed her on the throne. Lady Jane, the modest and learned girl who had been queen of England for nine days, was executed six months later.

Lady Jane Grey. Detail from a panel painting attributed to Master John.
NATIONAL PORTRAIT GALLERY

Edward VI. Anamorphosis, or distorted perspective painting to be viewed from the side, by William Scrots, 1546.
NATIONAL PORTRAIT GALLERY

MARY I
Born 1516, reigned 1553–1558

Mary was thirty-seven years old when she wrested the Crown from Northumberland in 1553. Her title to the succession had fluctuated throughout her life. Greeted with joy by her parents as their first healthy living child, she was betrothed at the age of two, as Henry's heiress-presumptive, to the newly born son of King Francis I of France. Showing her off to the French ambassador her proud father shouted in delight: 'By immortal God, Master Ambassador, this girl never cries!' At the age of nine in 1525 she was sent, with a huge and impressive suite, as her father's representative into the Welsh Marches, and was recalled to court early in 1527 to be shown off as the prospective bride in another French alliance, this time with King Francis himself. At the elaborate celebrations Mary pronounced speeches of welcome in both Latin and French to the French delegation, played for them on the virginals and danced for them in a masque with her ladies. This state of affairs came to an abrupt end when Henry, in his efforts to obtain a divorce or annulment, declared his marriage to Catherine of Aragon to be invalid because of her previous marriage to his brother, pronounced Mary illegitimate and out of the succession, and sent Mary and her mother away from court. Mary had to wait in this uncertain position until, after her mother's death, Henry's marriage to Jane Seymour, and her reluctant acknowledgement of her father as supreme head of the Church of England, she was allowed to return to Court in 1537. The birth of a male heir, the future Edward VI, weakened the claims of Henry's two daughters to the throne. For the remainder of her father's reign, and during that of her brother whom she held in great affection, Mary lived the life of a court lady, indulged by the Protestant Edward who allowed her to have her private mass and on friendly terms with two of her father's wives, Anne of Cleves and Catherine Parr.

Her personal popularity, combined with her gallant action in defeating the ambitious and unprincipled Northumberland carried her to the throne on a

Mary I. Panel painting by Hans Eworth, 1554. NATIONAL PORTRAIT GALLERY

wave of widespread enthusiasm, but this was soon dissipated. Mary's obstinate resolve to reinstate the Catholic Church as quickly as possible, and her insistence, against all advice, on marrying the son of Charles V, Philip of Spain, brought home to her dismayed subjects the realisation that their queen's actions had not only delivered them again into the hands of an external religious authority but had reduced England to a vassal of Spain. In 1557, dragged by Philip into his war against France, England lost Calais, her only remaining Continental possession.

Mary's violent persecution of Protestants – some three hundred victims, including Archbishop Cranmer, perished at the stake in four years – earned her the lasting epithet of 'Bloody Mary' and caused more and more of her despairing subjects to pin their hopes on her sister, Elizabeth, waiting quietly in the wings. In 1558 the happy little 'girl who never cries' died of a dropsical complaint (mistaken for pregnancy), childless, neglected by her husband and hated by her subjects, a bitterly disappointed and unhappy woman.

Philip II, King of Spain, husband of Mary I. Panel painting, unknown artist, c.1580. NATIONAL PORTRAIT GALLERY

ELIZABETH I
Born 1533, reigned 1558–1603

When Elizabeth came to the throne in 1558 she had already, rather like her grandfather Henry VII, passed through some twenty-odd turbulent years in which her fortunes had ebbed and flowed. Welcoming her somewhat grudgingly as a daughter instead of the longed-for son, Henry VIII had nevertheless granted the baby Elizabeth the full honours of a splendid ceremonial christening where Garter King-of-Arms proclaimed her style: 'God of his infinite goodness, sent prosperous life and long to the high and mighty Princess of England, Elizabeth!', and the setting up of a separate household. This last circumstance meant that the baby saw her mother, Anne Boleyn, only rarely, and was thus spared the grief and tragedy of Anne's execution when Elizabeth was still under three years old.

Pronounced illegitimate prior to her mother's death, Elizabeth joined her sister Mary in exclusion from the throne and from court. But the birth of their brother Edward brought about a general reconciliation. Elizabeth and Mary took part in Edward's christening ceremonies in October 1537. Elizabeth carried the richly embroidered baptismal robe, although because she was so tiny she herself had to be carried by two noblemen. From then on all three motherless children became the king's 'dearest children'. When in 1544 Henry caused Parliament to pass an act re-establishing the two girls in the succession, their alleged illegitimacy was no longer an issue. Mary of course was long past her schoolroom days, but Elizabeth and Edward, both precocious, intelligent and quick-witted children, underwent the intensive liberal education applied at the time to royal children whether boys or girls, exchanging letters in Latin and French and developing a close affection. Elizabeth's tutor, Roger Ascham, who was still reading Greek and Latin with her every day after she became queen, described the achievements of his pupil to a fellow scholar: 'Her study of true religion and learning is most eager. She talks French and Italian as well as she does English, and has often talked to me readily and well in Latin'.

In 1549 the peace of the schoolroom was shattered and Elizabeth placed in great danger when Thomas Seymour, widower of Catherine Parr and brother of Protector Somerset, who was dabbling in conspiracies against the protector and his council, made her the object of his gallantries. Seymour, arrested and placed in the Tower, was later executed, and Elizabeth was closely interrogated but escaped unscathed. Her caution on that occasion stood in her good stead during the turbulent days following the death of Edward VI. Standing aloof from Northumberland's ambitious conspiracy involving his daughter-in-law Lady Jane Grey, Elizabeth supported Mary and rode behind her sister when the latter made her ceremonial entry into London as queen on 3 August 1553. Elizabeth's fortunes swung from one extreme to another during the five years of Mary's troubled reign; at first in favour and at court, she was soon passing through the Traitors' Gate to be imprisoned in the Tower on charges of conspiracy, only to be released after two months for lack of evidence. Confined to various country

FAR LEFT
Elizabeth I. Miniature by Nicholas Hilliard, 1572.
NATIONAL PORTRAIT GALLERY

LEFT
Elizabeth I. Panel painting attributed to Nicholas Hilliard, c.1572–6. Known as the 'Pelican Portrait' because the queen wears a jewelled pelican at her breast.
WALKER ART GALLERY

ABOVE RIGHT
Elizabeth I. Panel painting by Marcus Gheeraerts the Younger, c.1592.
NATIONAL PORTRAIT GALLERY

houses, with intermittent returns to court where Mary constantly strove to convert her sister to Catholicism, Elizabeth was gradually becoming the focus of the hopes and dreams of those anxious to be rid of the imposition by Mary of Spanish, and Papal, domination. Courtiers and counsellors were already collecting about the future queen – among them Sir William Cecil who, as Lord Burghley, would be her chief adviser for over forty years – when, on 17 November 1558, news was brought to Elizabeth at Hatfield House that Mary was dead.

The joyful enthusiasm with which the majority of her subjects greeted the new queen, and the love and admiration they displayed, lasted wellnigh through her reign of almost forty-five years. This can largely be attributed to Elizabeth's personality. Combining the caution and levelheadedness of her grandfather Henry VII with the dash, energy and charm of her father, Elizabeth steered a calculated course in domestic and foreign policy, employing the 'balance-of-power' tactics used by Henry VIII to such effect that King Henry IV of France could exclaim, towards the end of her reign: 'She alone is a King! She alone knows how to rule!', and Pope Sixtus V could declare, in 1588: 'She certainly is a great Queen . . . Just look how well she governs! She is only a woman, only mistress of half an island, and yet she makes herself feared by Spain, by France, by the Empire, by all'. The Pope's words, 'only a woman', epitomise the difficulties of the sixteenth-century woman ruler which Mary failed to resolve but which Elizabeth was able to overcome: the yardstick by which she was judged was how closely her behaviour approximated to that of a king. When tutor Ascham wanted to praise Elizabeth he wrote: 'Her mind has no womanly weakness, her perseverance is equal to that of a man'. Elizabeth evinced an intelligent perception of her dual role as king and queen. She perfectly understood the need to display the 'masculine' qualities of strength, warlike ardour and

statecraft, for example, in the speech she made to her army on the eve of the expected Armada invasion: 'I know I have the body of a weak and feeble woman, but I have the heart and stomach of a King . . .' At the same time, she gave free rein to the 'womanly' attributes of compassion and pity, for example, by feeding her aged counsellor Burghley during his last illness 'with her own princely hand, as a careful nurse'.

In taking on this dual role Elizabeth tacitly ruled out marriage. Until her accession every female monarch was expected to find a husband, and indeed throughout her reign this question was discussed endlessly by her subjects, by her male counsellors – who earnestly debated the queen's ability to bear children until well past the accepted age – and by the queen herself. Of all the many suitors for her hand only the Duke of Alençon, youngest son of King Henry II of France, would appear to have found favour in the eyes of Elizabeth, who was amused by his persistent courtship. That he was over twenty years younger and pock-marked into the bargain were forgotten when, throwing pride and protocol to the winds, he crossed secretly from France in 1579 to see her. Elizabeth had to give way, however, to the vociferous opposition to the match of

her subjects and her Council. In 1582 she saw her 'Frog', as she nicknamed him, off after his final visit to her, travelling with him and the whole Court as far as Canterbury, showing him her fleet of ships, sending a large train of distinguished courtiers and gentlemen to accompany him to the Netherlands, and honouring him as if in fact he had been her accepted husband. The political repercussions of this protracted though unsuccessful courtship served Elizabeth well by frightening Spain with the prospect of an English–French alliance and by keeping England from being too embroiled in war in the Netherlands. But she sincerely mourned her 'Frog' when news of his death from fever arrived in June 1584: 'Melancholy does so possess us', wrote one of her Council, 'as both public and private causes are at a stay for a season'.

The long-standing threat posed by the claim of Mary Queen of Scots to the throne of England through her grandmother Margaret, sister of Henry VIII, was finally disposed of in 1587. Initial efforts at friendship between the two queens had not survived the disasters of the Scottish queen's stormy reign. Deposed by her nobles in 1567 in favour of her infant son James VI, she eventually fled to England where, kept in custody, she inevitably became the focus of English Catholicism. Her unhappy story ended when her suspected implication in the Babington conspiracy to murder Elizabeth brought her to the scaffold on a charge of treason.

The Elizabethan era witnessed England becoming united, strong and wealthy, the consolidation of Protestantism as the state religion, and the steady growth of nationalism – Elizabeth herself boasted that she was 'descended by father and mother of mere English blood'. The resounding defeat of the attempted invasion of England in 1588 by the huge fleet of the Spanish Armada demonstrated to Continental powers England's mastery of the seas and promoted her trade and overseas expansion.

In the cultured atmosphere of Elizabeth's court, music, literature and the arts, particularly portraiture, flourished. Just as her father had received his enduring image from the hand of Holbein, so his daughter's royal face was immortalised by Nicholas Hilliard who was Elizabeth's goldsmith, limner, painter of portraits 'in large' and especially of portraits 'in little', the exquisite minatures which encapsulate the cultured elegance, refined charm, talented high spirits and sentimental moments of Elizabeth's Renaissance court. Tutor Ascham had observed of his pupil: 'She delights as much in music as she is skilful in it', and one of Hilliard's most intimately perceptive miniatures shows Elizabeth playing her lute. It was said of Hilliard by a contemporary that he had studied the queen's face so closely that he could render her likeness with four strokes of his pencil. In his *Treatise on the Arte of Limning* Hilliard describes Elizabeth's knowledge of painting, her dislike of the technique of shadowing in portraits, and her opinion that the best place for a sitter was 'in the open alley of a goodly garden, where no tree was neere, nor any shadowe at all . . .'. The queen received miniatures from, and gave them to, her favourite courtiers. One of herself in a tiny manuscript prayerbook was prepared as a gift for her suitor, the Duke of Alençon. She wore the elaborate 'picture boxes', as they were sometimes called, pinned to her dress, at her waist, on her elbow and once, for a jest, on her shoe. The image of this most popular of all 'royal faces', in portraits proliferating from officially approved 'patterns' by Hilliard and many other court painters, was to be seen everywhere during the sixteenth century, in courts abroad and in country house galleries at home, and has become imprinted for ever in England's history.

When it became obvious that Queen Elizabeth would bear no children, the question of who was to succeed her became of desperate importance to her subjects, her Council and to the House of Commons. Elizabeth, constantly urged by them all to name her successor, refused to do so, but let it be known during her last years that her choice had fallen on King James VI of Scotland, the only son of Mary Queen of Scots.

Elizabeth's long reign with its many changing social patterns – in particular the rise of a new prosperous middle class which made up more and more of the House of Commons and was beginning to feel its power – came to an end in the early hours of 24 March 1603. As England's 'Gloriana' passed quietly away, a horseman was riding hard to Edinburgh to bring the news of the queen's death to her successor, King James VI of Scotland, now King James I of England.

ABOVE *Elizabeth I. Engraving by Crispin van de Passe the Elder, after Isaac Oliver.* NATIONAL PORTRAIT GALLERY

RIGHT *Elizabeth I. Panel painting by or after George Gower, c.1588, commemorating the defeat of the Spanish Armada.* NATIONAL PORTRAIT GALLERY

JAMES I
Born 1566, reigned 1603–1625

James was the great-grandson of Margaret Tudor, sister of Henry VIII. By her first marriage to King James IV of Scotland, she had a son, James V; by her second marriage to the Earl of Angus she had a daughter, Lady Margaret Douglas, who married the Earl of Lennox. James V's only legitimate child was Mary Queen of Scots; the Earl and Countess of Lennox had a son, Henry Lord Darnley. The marriage of Mary Queen of Scots and Darnley – who both stood in line for the throne of England – produced one son, James VI of Scotland who, inheriting his parents' joint claim to the throne of England, succeeded Elizabeth in 1603 as James I of England.

When James acceded to the throne he was thirty-seven years old, had been married to Anne of Denmark since 1589 and was the father of three surviving children, Henry (named after his grandfather Darnley and Henry VII) aged nine, Elizabeth (named to compliment Queen Elizabeth) aged seven and Charles aged three. James had been proclaimed King of Scotland when he was one year old, following his mother's forced abdication and subsequent confinement in England. He grew up in a turmoil of faction and struggles by his Scottish nobles to gain control of his person, and three of the four regents appointed during his childhood came to violent ends. Through all these upheavals he was subjected to a rigorous regime of study and discipline. One of his tutors was the famous scholar George Buchanan, another was Peter Young, trained in Calvinist Geneva. James was an apt pupil, speaking Latin and French with ease at the age of eight – although he complained that he had been made to speak Latin before he could converse in Scots – and receiving a thorough grounding in Protestant theology.

As he grew up his hopes of escaping from his warring nobles and scolding ministers rested upon his being named as Elizabeth's successor. To this end he made only formal protests in 1587 when his beautiful but tragic mother, caught in the web of her pathetic intrigues, was sentenced to death in England. When at last, in 1603, the summons to England came, James set off joyfully, progressing to his new capital through cheering crowds of well-wishers and greeted by English courtiers who had ridden out to meet him on the way. This euphoria of his new subjects was due in part to a feeling of relief that the succession had been settled at last and that James, although founding a Stuart dynasty, was a descendant of the Tudor line, and was also due in part to the fact that he was a staunch Protestant and had already had experience of ruling.

James I in robes of state. Oil painting by Daniel Mytens, 1621. NATIONAL PORTRAIT GALLERY

The euphoria was short-lived as, in spite of the above and other qualities, James was unable to come to terms with the new spirit in the English Parliament. His intentions of maintaining peace by non-interference abroad, imposing unity in the Church and achieving a complete union of his two kingdoms foundered when the English Parliament put forward its claim, previously rejected by Queen Elizabeth, to give advice on foreign and Church policies.

The timely discovery of the Roman Catholic Guy Fawkes plot to blow up the king and the two Houses of Parliament in 1605 only temporarily calmed the antagonism between James and his Commons. In 1613 James married his daughter Elizabeth to Frederick, the Elector Palatine who, by accepting in 1619 the throne of Protestant Bohemia, brought upon himself and his wife, 'The Winter Queen', defeat and exile at the hands of the Hapsburgs. In 1621 James was contemplating a match for his son Charles with the Spanish Infanta, and asked Parliament for funds to restore Frederick with Spanish help. The Commons refused the money, condemned the proposed marriage and proposed that Spain itself should be attacked. In a fury James dissolved Parliament, arrested several members and ripped

Henry, Prince of Wales, eldest son of James I. Miniature by Isaac Oliver, c.1612.
ROYAL COLLECTION

their page of protestations out of the Commons' journal. However, a disastrous and humiliating incognito trip to Spain by Charles and his father's favourite, the Duke of Buckingham, in pursuit of the Infanta, so unnerved James that he made an alliance with the Dutch and prepared for hostilities against Spain. James died in 1625 (and his funeral was as magnificent and disorderly as his court had been), leaving to his son Charles the legacy of imminent war and an ongoing struggle with Parliament.

James's interests were literary rather than artistic. He was the author of several books including poetry, psalm translations, treatises on theological matters and the *Basilikon Doron* expounding his views on the divine right of kings, and is notably remembered for his sponsorship of the 'King James', or 'Authorised Version' of the Bible completed in 1611. Yet he understood the need for state portraits and retained Nicholas Hilliard as one of his court painters. But it was the hand of Hilliard's successor, Isaac Oliver, which preserved for posterity the most striking of the reign's 'royal faces' – that of James's eldest son, Prince Henry, the enthusiastic young patron of the arts who died, mourned by all, in 1612.

When Prince Henry died Charles was twelve years old and had lived until then in the shadow of his brilliant and popular brother. As he grew up he fell under the influence of his father's favourite, the Duke of Buckingham who, as Lord High Admiral, engaged in disastrous exploits. These discredited Charles as king and embittered his relations with Parliament; as in his father's reign the royal prerogative to decide foreign policy was questioned. Charles's marriage to Henrietta Maria, daughter of King Henry IV of France, re-awakened fears that Roman Catholicism, the bride's religion, would again become all-powerful.

Although the hated Buckingham's influence ended with his assassination in 1628, Parliament, summoned in 1629, continued to defy the king, refusing his demands for money and insisting on debating religious matters. Charles's reply was to dissolve Parliament and rule without it for the next eleven years. When his eforts to bring Scotland's Calvinist Church closer to the Church of England had provoked a Scottish uprising, he was forced to summon Parliament in 1640 to demand finances for his subsequent military expedition. Rejecting this demand, the 'Short Parliament' was immediately dissolved, but not before one of its members, John Pym, had pronounced, on the floor of the House, these memorable words: 'The powers of Parliament are to the body politic as the rational faculties of the soul to man'. The 'Long Parliament', summoned in the same year, antagonised the desperate king who retaliated by entering the Commons with his armed followers in an illegal attempt to arrest Pym and four other members; forewarned, they sought sanctuary in London's City. Charles's imprudent act irrevocably widened the breach between king and Commons and unleashed the Civil War. The Royalists' early successes turned into utter defeat after the Battle of Naseby was decisively won by Oliver Cromwell's New Model Army. Subsequent events brought Charles himself to the scaffold and the Crown into abeyance in 1649.

Anne of Denmark, Queen of James I. Panel painting attributed to William Larkin, c.1612.
NATIONAL PORTRAIT GALLERY

Charles's absolute belief in the divine right of kings imperilled the Crown, but his intelligent and enthusiastic interest in art, and especially in 'royal faces', formed for his descendants the nucleus of an unsurpassed Royal Collection. Charles had groups of miniatures of his ancestors and family displayed in his Cabinet Room at Whitehall. He hung a series of full-length portraits of his forebears, his queen and royal in-laws – completing it with posthumous pictures of his father and Prince Henry – in the Cross Gallery at Somerset House. He commissioned Rubens to paint the ceiling of the Banqueting House at Whitehall and, above all, he brought Van Dyck to England to transform the royal portrait. Van Dyck's continental experience and brilliant technique produced state portraits of unsurpassed splendour, setting a pattern of style and elegance for years to come; his strangely haunting triple portrait of Charles, originally intended merely as a pattern for a bust by the sculptor Bernini, has become an indelible image of that unhappy king.

Charles I in three positions. By Sir Anthony Van Dyck, c.1635. ROYAL COLLECTION

The five eldest children of Charles I. Left to right: Mary, James (later James II), Charles (later Charles II), Elizabeth and Anne. After Sir Anthony Van Dyck, 1637. NATIONAL PORTRAIT GALLERY

Henrietta Maria, Queen of Charles I. After Sir Anthony Van Dyck, c.1632–5. NATIONAL PORTRAIT GALLERY

THE INTERREGNUM
1649–1660

CHARLES II
Born 1630, reigned 1660–1685

When, watched by a completely silent crowd of Londoners, Charles I stepped out of the window of the Whitehall Banqueting Hall on to the scaffold on a wintry morning in January 1649, and laid his head on the block, his execution ushered in a period of eleven years without a monarchy. The uneasy and unworkable balance between King and Commons was dissolved to give the Parliamentary, or rather the Roundhead, Party, supreme power. Under Oliver Cromwell's personal rule as Lord Protector, the Commonwealth Government controlled the Army, enlarged the Navy and imposed taxation to a degree unknown to any Stuart king, displaying an efficiency which impressed foreign nations.

But such a concentration of power in one party and its leader, based not on consent but on force, could not be sustained after the leader's death. Cromwell's dynastic ambitions led him to name as his successor his son Richard who proved quite unfit to wield the sword as his father had done. Army mutinies forced the election of the Convention Parliament of 1660, whose members, a mix of moderate Roundheads and Royalists, recalled the eldest son of the martyred king to ascend the throne as Charles II.

Portraiture during the Interregnum was almost completely unaffected by political events. Whether Cromwell's supposed injunction to his painter to portray him 'warts and all' was a sincere expression of his aesthetic beliefs or an affectation designed to promote his image as a bluff 'no-nonsense' type of man, it made no difference to the painters who continued to follow the modes of Charles I's day. Robert Walker, who portrayed many of the leading Commonwealth men, simply adapted styles and poses from earlier pictures, especially those by Van Dyck. Cromwell's possible inclination to become a 'royal face' himself can be glimpsed in his elaborately regal funeral ceremonies (closely modelled on those of King James I in 1625), where his medieval-type effigy lay in state under a crown.

Charles was thirty years old when he was invited to return to London to resume the Crown, and his life until then had been full of contrasts. Welcomed with delight by Charles I and his wife Henrietta Maria – 'You are the child of our love', his father later affirmed – he was brought up as heir to the throne, given his own household at the age of eight and carefully educated, only to be thrown into the turmoil of the Civil War and appointed as captain-general for his father in the west country before he was fifteen. By 1646 the defeated Royalist army had become too dangerous a place for the heir to the throne and Charles was sent to safety in France. After his father's execution he made various abortive attempts to regain his kingdom. Landing in Scotland he was crowned King of Scots after signing an agreement with the Covenanters, and advanced with an army into England. His defeat by a Commonwealth force at Worcester in 1651 forced him to flee again to the Continent, where he spent his time 'on his travels', as he described his wanderings around Europe seeking help to regain his throne.

Charles's triumphant entry into his heritage without force, without foreign aid and without conditions was the prelude to a reign in which the struggle between king and Parliament in the disputed areas of foreign policy and religion was to be replayed. Leaving Parliament to solve the thorny problem of resettlement of Crown, Church and Royalist lands appropriated by the Commonwealth, Charles pursued a secret and tortuous foreign policy dictated by the actions of his neighbours, his Protestant Dutch nephew William III of Orange and the warmongering Catholic King Louis XIV of France. His marriage to the Catholic Portuguese princess, Catherine of Braganza, raised the old fears of a Catholic heir. But Catherine was childless, and Charles soothed these fears by insisting that Mary and Anne, daughters of his heir, his brother James, be brought up as Protestants, and eventually ensured the Protestant succession by marrying Mary to William III of

Charles II as a young man. Miniature on vellum, by David des Granges after Adriaen Hanneman, c.1648.
NATIONAL PORTRAIT GALLERY

Catherine of Braganza, Queen of Charles II. Oil painting by or after Dirk Stoop, c.1660–1.
NATIONAL PORTRAIT GALLERY

Orange and Anne to Prince George of Denmark.

Charles I's picture collection had been dispersed during the Commonwealth. His son reassembled as many as he could, placing most of them in the long Stone Gallery at Whitehall, which he opened to the public. Charles himself had been portrayed from infancy, though his mother, writing to a friend when he was four months old, apologised: 'I will send you his portrait as soon as he is a little fairer, for at present he is so dark that I am ashamed of him'. But Charles remained 'so dark' and was nicknamed the Black Boy. As well as being a patron of the arts, Charles encouraged the sciences, founding the Royal Society, and the Royal Observatory at Greenwich. His private life was a continual source of interest to his subjects; of his thirteen illegitimate children five of his sons were present at his death-bed. But his failure to produce a legitimate heir plunged the country into religious turmoil when Catholic James became King in 1685.

James, three years younger than Charles II, had shared his exile on the Continent, spending his time as he grew up in fighting for various causes – first in the Fronde wars in France where he distinguished himself as a general under Marshall Turenne and then in the Spanish army. Appointed Lord High Admiral by Charles II after the Restoration in 1660, James displayed a well-informed interest in naval matters, as the diaries of Pepys, then Admiralty Secretary, confirm. In the same year he married his Protestant mistress Anne Hyde, daughter of Charles's chief minister Edward, Earl of Clarendon – a marriage that was deplored by the bride's father

James II. Miniature by Samuel Cooper. VICTORIA & ALBERT MUSEUM

Charles II, in coronation robes. Painting by John Michael Wright, 1661. ROYAL COLLECTION

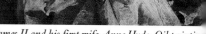

James II and his first wife, Anne Hyde. Oil painting,

and the groom's mother but supported by the king. The two daughters of this marriage, Mary and Anne, were brought up as Protestants and both became queens of England. After the death of his first wife in 1671 James, now a declared Catholic, married a Catholic Italian princess, Mary of Modena, who was still childless when James became king in 1685.

The first months of James's reign witnessed an attempt by the Protestant Duke of Monmouth, eldest and favourite illegitimate son of Charles II, to seize the Crown from James, a revolt put down by military force against the duke who perished on the scaffold, and by legal means against his followers under the brutal hand of Judge Jeffreys. This abortive revolt gave James an excuse to keep a standing army of some 30,000 men. He established a large army camp on Hounslow Heath to hold London in check, and pressed on with his plans to bring the country back to Catholicism by claiming the royal prerogative to suspend Parliament's laws. In the face of this double assault on their

James II. Oil painting by Sir Godfrey Kneller, 1684–5. NATIONAL PORTRAIT GALLERY

Peter Lely, 1660s. NATIONAL PORTRAIT GALLERY

religion and Parliamentary privileges, his dismayed subjects turned to the Protestant hero of Europe, William III of Orange, James's nephew and husband of his elder daughter Mary. The unexpected birth of a son to James and Mary of Modena in June 1688, with its im-plication that the Catholic line would prevail, galvanised the country into action. James contributed to his own downfall by fleeing to France with his wife and baby son, and William and Mary were invited to occupy the throne as joint rulers.

WILLIAM III AND MARY II

William III born 1650, reigned 1688–1702   *Mary II born 1662, reigned 1688–1694*

By arranging the marriage in 1677 of his fifteen-year-old niece Mary to her twenty-seven-year-old cousin William of Orange, Europe's most popular anti-French Protestant leader, Charles II hoped to calm his subjects' fears both of French aggression and of a Catholic dynasty. For his part William hoped to draw England into his alliance against France, an ambition not fully realised until he and Mary were invited to become king and queen in 1688, in an event known as the 'Glorious Revolution' because of its bloodless and peaceful nature.

After dealing with James II's attempted invasion of Ireland to recover his Crown, by defeating him decisively at the Battle of the Boyne in 1690, William devoted most of his time and energy to campaigning until the Peace of Ryswick, in 1697, brought a short respite in the wars against France.

Mary died of smallpox in 1694 at the early age of thirty-two while the war was at its height. Her marriage, which had started unhappily – she is said to have cried for a day and a half when told her destiny – and which remained childless, developed into a companionable relationship. Mary shared with William strong religious faith and a sense of duty, as well as an interest in architecture, interior decoration and gardens. The appointment of Sir Christopher Wren as their Surveyor-General led to the build-

Mary II. Oil painting, after William Wissing.
NATIONAL PORTRAIT GALLERY

William III. Attributed to Thomas Murray.   NATIONAL PORTRAIT GALLERY

ANNE
Born 1665, reigned 1702–1714

William III and Mary II. Detail from an engraving by C Allard after R de Hooghe's illustration for a Dutch broadsheet. BRITISH MUSEUM

Three days after her accession Queen Anne addressed Parliament. Her words: 'As I know my heart to be entirely English, I can very sincerely assure you that there is not one thing you can expect or desire of me which I shall not be ready to do for the happiness or prosperity of England . . .', delivered in her clear musical voice with becoming dignity, were greeted with enthusiasm and set the standard for her conscientious fulfilment of the duties of a monarch. Her reign of twelve years was almost wholly occupied with carrying on William III's war against France. Anne appointed the Duke of Marlborough, husband of her favourite Sarah Jennings, as supreme commander and his string of victories – Blenheim, Ramillies, Oudenarde and Malplaquet – delighted the nation.

The Treaty of Utrecht in 1713 brought many gains to Britain, not least being her overseas acquisitions from France in the New World. The colonisation, in Elizabeth I's reign, of Newfoundland in 1583 and Virginia in 1584, followed in James I's reign by the *Mayflower* pilgrims' landfall in New England in 1620, were only the start of a huge expansion in exploration, colonisation ing of Kensington Palace, the refurbishment of Hampton Court and its gardens and the introduction into England of the popular Dutch style of gardening. William was heart-broken at Mary's death and never remarried.

The domestic repercussions of the 'Glorious Revolution' were far-reaching: the Bill of Rights presented to Mary and William on their accession laid the basis for constitutional monarchy; the 1701 Act of Settlement decided the succession and laid down, among other conditions, that every future monarch must be a member of the Church of England. The political parties of Tories and Whigs which had slowly developed from the former 'Court' and 'Country' parties of the start of Charles II's reign, were growing in strength and influence. The need for money to finance William's wars led to Parliament gradually taking over financial arrangements and, in 1694, to the foundation of the Bank of England which attracted considerable Dutch investment and, in later reigns, was to make London the financial capital of Europe. William died in 1702 after a riding accident, leaving to his successor, his sister-in-law Anne, the troubled legacy of an imminent war with France.

Queen Anne. Oil painting, studio of John Closterman, c.1702. NATIONAL PORTRAIT GALLERY

Queen Anne and the Knights of the Garter. Oil painting by Peter Angelis, c.1713. NATIONAL PORTRAIT GALLERY

GEORGE I
Born 1660, reigned 1714–1727

George I, who established the House of Hanover on the English throne, was fifty-four years old when he became king. His inability to speak English, his absences in Hanover and his general lack of interest in English affairs promoted the growth of constitutional government. However, George insisted that his ministers should belong to the Whig Party, subscribing to the general belief that the Tories favoured the Jacobite claim, although the ill-planned – and quickly suppressed – Jacobite rising in Scotland in 1715, intended to place the 'Old Pretender' on the throne, received little English support. Sir Robert Walpole, who had held office in Queen Anne's reign but resigned in 1710 when the Tories came to power, managed to restore national credit and confidence in 1720 in the 'South Sea Bubble' crisis caused by the mania for speculation, and then remained in office for some twenty years during which the country enjoyed a period of peace.

George I did not bring his queen, Sophia Dorothea, to England. Suspecting an adulterous liaison, he had her confined at the age of twenty-eight in the Castle of Ahlden for the rest of her life and forbade her to see her children, one of whom was the future George II. Sophia died in 1726. In the following year George, travelling to arrange her funeral, suffered a heart attack and was buried in Hanover.

State portraiture had been in the capable hands of the German-born painter, Sir Godfrey Kneller, for five reigns, providing a vivid illustration of the royal faces of the period. Appointed principal painter to Charles II in 1678, his portraits of George I earned him a baronetcy in 1715.

and trade which culminated in the first British Empire. The Union of the Parliaments of Scotland and England, so much desired by Anne's great-grandfather James I, took place in 1707, and her reign also witnessed the rising power of the House of Commons, the birth of the modern newspaper and of the provincial press.

In 1683 Anne had been married to the Lutheran Prince George of Denmark; her seventeen pregnancies produced only one child, the little Duke of Gloucester who died aged eleven in 1700 before she became queen. 'Good Queen Anne', ruler of what Daniel Defoe called 'the most flourishing and opulent country in the world', died in 1714, at the age of forty-nine, prematurely aged and worn out with illness. 'I believe sleep was never more welcome to a weary traveller than death was to her', wrote her doctor of the last monarch of the House of Stuart.

The death of Anne's only child, the Duke of Gloucester, in 1700 prompted Parliament to pass in 1701 the Act of Settlement whereby the succession to the throne was decided: should Anne die without issue the Crown would go to the Protestant grandchild of James I, Sophia (daughter of Elizabeth 'the Winter Queen' and the Elector Palatine Frederick, King of Bohemia) and to her issue. Sophia, who had married the Elector of Hanover and had a son George, died a few months before Anne in 1714, and the Crown therefore passed to her son who came to the throne as George I of the House of Hanover. The clause in the Act of Settlement requiring that the monarch must belong to the Church of England automatically excluded the Catholic descendants of the deposed King James II, both his son James Francis Edward Stuart, known as 'the Old Pretender', and the latter's son, Charles Edward Stuart, known as 'the Young Pretender' or 'Bonnie Prince Charlie'.

Queen Anne and Prince George of Denmark, by Charles Boit, 1706. ROYAL COLLECTION

RIGHT
George I. Oil painting by Sir Godfrey Kneller, 1716.
NATIONAL PORTRAIT GALLERY

GEORGE II
Born 1683, reigned 1727–1760

When George II became King in 1727 he was forty-four years old, had been married to Caroline of Anspach since 1705 and had eight children. George, whose interest in English affairs was almost as limited as his father's had been, retained Sir Robert Walpole as his chief minister until the latter resigned in 1742 after England's participation in the War of the Austrian Succession. George himself, aged sixty, on foot and sword in hand, led the Hanoverian and English infantry into action against the French at Dettingen in 1743 – the last time an English monarch commanded his troops on the field of battle. George's second son, the Duke of Cumberland, accompanied him on the campaign. In 1745, a Jacobite rising to place on the throne the grandson of James II, the gallant and popular young Bonnie Prince Charlie, was brutally put down by Cumberland after the Battle of Culloden in a punitive campaign which earned him the name of 'Butcher', and which extinguished for ever the Jacobite threat to the Hanoverian dynasty. When George II died, aged seventy-seven, his reign ended in a blaze of glory; under the inspired ministry of

Caroline of Anspach, Queen of George II.
Oil painting, studio of Charles Jervas, c.1727.

William Pitt the Elder, known as 'the Great Commoner', Britain emerged supreme from the Seven Years' War having destroyed French power in India and in Canada.

George delighted in music and opera, continuing his father's patronage of Handel. Queen Caroline's interests were artistic – in her closet at Kensington she arranged miniatures, little paintings and drawings, some of them by Holbein, to form her personal exhibition of royal faces. George's devotion to his queen, who predeceased him in 1737, found expression in his will – he ordered that, in their joint sarcophagus in Westminster Abbey, the adjoining sides of their wooden coffins be removed to allow their dust to mingle after death.

George II's eldest son, Frederick Prince of Wales, was born in 1707 in Hanover and came to England in 1728. In 1736 he married Princess Augusta of Saxe-Gotha and they had seven children. Frederick was a discerning patron of the arts, commissioning work from gold- and silver-smiths, taking an active part in the establishment of the Vauxhall Pleasure Gardens where he had his private pavilion, and employing a number of English and foreign portrait painters. Frederick predeceased his father, dying in 1751. When George II died in 1760 he was succeeded by his grandson, Frederick's eldest son, who came to the throne as George III.

Frederick, Prince of Wales, liked to be known as the 'Patriot Prince', and his son, George III, followed this lead when, addressing his first Parliament, he proudly declared: 'Born and educated in this country, I glory in the name of Briton', a nostalgic echo of Elizabeth I's 'mere English' and Queen Anne's 'entirely English'. The twenty-three-year-old George married seventeen year old Princess Charlotte of Mecklenburg-Strelitz in 1761, and for the first time in many years the 'royal faces' were young ones.

George's determination during the first twenty years of his reign to revive the powers of the Crown by reducing ministers and Cabinet to servants of the king and controlling the Commons by patronage, led to confused government and the War of American Independence whereby Britain lost her thirteen colonies, became embroiled with France and Spain and was near to forfeiting her mastery of the seas. Accepting personal defeat and renouncing political power for the Crown, in 1784 George invited twenty-four-year-old William Pitt 'the Younger', son of Pitt 'the Elder' to become his prime minister, an office which Pitt held, apart from one short break, until his death.

Pitt inaugurated a period of peace and stability until the consequences of the French Revolution, the events of the Terror and the execution of King Louis

LEFT *George II. Oil painting, studio of Charles Jervas, c.1727.* NATIONAL PORTRAIT GALLERY

BELOW *George III, Queen Charlotte and six of their children (left to right): Prince William (later William IV), George, Prince of Wales (later George IV) with Prince Frederick (later Duke of York), Prince Edward (later Duke of Kent), Princess Charlotte and Princess Augusta. Oil painting by Johan Zoffany, 1770.* ROYAL COLLECTION

Queen Charlotte, wife of George III. Enamel miniature on copper by Henry Bone, 1801.
NATIONAL PORTRAIT GALLERY

XVI, plunged Britain in 1793 into a twenty-year-long war with France. After initial reverses the tide began to turn in 1805 with the naval victory of Nelson, 'England's Hero', at Trafalgar. In the following year the worn-out Pitt, aged forty-seven, died, proclaiming confidently: 'England has saved herself by her exertions and will, I trust, save Europe by her example'. England's second Hero, the Duke of Wellington, finally brought the war to a victorious conclusion with the defeat of Napoleon at the Battle of Waterloo in 1815, but victory came too late to be appreciated by the king, lost in his private world of what was then considered madness, now suggested by modern medical opinion to be the disease porphyria. George's

George III in uniform. Studio of Sir William Beechey, c.1800. NATIONAL PORTRAIT GALLERY

eldest son, later George IV, acted as his regent from 1811 to 1820. George III's interest in agriculture, which earned him the nickname of 'Farmer George', led to the setting-up of his model farm near Windsor Castle, a favourite residence of the king and queen and their large family.

Both George and Charlotte patronised portrait painters extensively. Windsor was a favourite setting for informal family group portraits by, among others, Benjamin West and Zoffany. The latter is said to have complained ruefully of the difficulty of completing royal family groups because of the regular arrival of new members of the family – Charlotte had fifteen children. George arranged a collection of royal portraits, including Zoffany's portraits of himself and Charlotte, in the Queen's Gallery at Kensington Palace and Jeremiah Meyer was appointed as miniature-painter to the queen, who favoured these tiny images of royal faces and frequently wore them.

LEFT   *George III. 'Temperance enjoying a Frugal Meal'. Cartoon by James Gillray, published in 1792.*
NATIONAL PORTRAIT GALLERY

GEORGE IV
Born 1762, regent 1811–1820, reigned 1820–1830

George IV is better known by his title of Prince Regent, conferred when his father, George III, became unfit to rule in 1811, and by his activities before and during the Regency, then by his ten years as king. His regency celebrated the end of the French Wars in 1815, which heralded a long period of stability abroad and momentous social changes at home. The new agricultural methods, the increase in factories, trade within the second British Empire of North America, India and the West Indies, the improvements in transport and the early days of railways and steam-ships were all bringing prosperity to the country as a whole, but creating at the same time a large population living at an unacceptable poverty level.

The prince regent's ostentatious and extravagent way of life aroused growing resentment, while the public manner in which his private life was conducted provoked an increasingly contemptuous disrespect for the monarchy. At the age of twenty-three George had contracted a secret, illegal marriage with a Roman Catholic widow, Mrs Fitzherbert. Ten years later in 1795 he was so overwhelmingly in debt that he agreed to an arranged marriage with his cousin Caroline of Brunswick if his debts were paid. But the marriage was not a success – before their daughter Charlotte was born in the following year the incompatible parents had separated and their subsequent doings until Caroline's death in 1821 were to provide endless ammunition for satirical cartoonists and political adversaries. Charlotte's marriage in 1816 to Prince Leopold of Saxe-Coburg reconciled father and daughter, but the death of both Charlotte and her baby in childbirth in 1817 served not only to increase the prince regent's unpopularity but brought up again the vexed question of his heir. Hastily arranged alliances for his unmarried brothers produced only one offspring, a daughter (the future Queen Victoria) born to the Duke of Kent and his wife in 1819.

George IV's expensive life-style (his coronation robes alone cost £24,000)

and his failings as a monarch were compensated for, to a certain extent in some contemporary eyes, by his generous and informed patronage of the arts. The Brighton Pavilion, London's Regent Park, Regent Street and the reconstructed Buckingham Palace all owe

RIGHT
George IV when Prince Regent Unfinished oil painting by Sir Thomas Lawrence, c.1814.
NATIONAL PORTRAIT GALLERY

BELOW
George IV. 'A Voluptuary under the horrors of Digestion'. Cartoon by James Gillray, published in 1792.
NATIONAL PORTRAIT GALLERY

A VOLUPTUARY under the horrors of Digestion.

WILLIAM IV
Born 1765, reigned 1830–1837

George IV, after Sir Thomas Lawrence's 1822 original. ROYAL COLLECTION

their existence to him, as do the alterations to Windsor Castle, the acquisitions by the British Museum of some 65,000 books from George III's library and of the Elgin Marbles, and the formation of a nucleus of a national picture collection. He encouraged writers (Sir Walter Scott considered him 'every inch a King' and Jane Austen dedicated her *Emma* to him), willingly displayed his own extensive collection of pictures, saying: 'I have not formed it for my own pleasure alone, but to gratify the public taste', and patronised numerous painters, notably Lawrence, whom he knighted in 1815. Nor did he forget his ancestors, commissioning a magnificent tomb by the sculptor Canova for James 'the Old Pretender' and his two sons, 'Bonnie Prince Charlie' and Henry, Cardinal York in St Peter's Rome – a graceful act of reconciliation of the Houses of Hanover and Stuart. Wellington's remark: 'that the nation would always have cause to be grateful to a man who had been a most magnificent patron of the arts in this country', and the French diplomat Prince Talleyrand's epitaph: 'he was *un roi grand seigneur*; there are no others left', aptly sum up the Regency age and its progenitor.

George IV's death in 1830 brought his brother William, Duke of Clarence, then aged sixty-five, to the throne. A long liaison with an actress, Mrs Jordan, had given William ten illegitimate children, the Fitzclarences, but his marriage, in 1818, to the young Princess Adelaide of Saxe-Meiningen had produced no living legitimate offspring. William's heir, therefore, was his little eleven-year-old niece Victoria, daughter of his brother the Duke of Kent. William entered the Navy at the age of fourteen and spent most of his life in the service, being present at the victory off Cape Saint Vincent in 1797. Fanny Burney, novelist and Assistant Keeper of the Robes to Queen Charlotte, gives an amusing picture of the 'Royal Sailor' – William, while attending a ball at St James's for his father's birthday in 1791, paid a jovial visit to his mother's attendants and insisting on treating them all, including Fanny, to champagne. A popular ballad of the beginning of William's reign entitled 'Our Queen is the wife of a sailor', underlines his liking to be depicted as the bluff 'Sailor King', a 'plain man' indulging in none of the extravagances of his brother George IV, and making himself accessible to his subjects. When his niece Victoria, at the start of her reign, discussed with her Prime Minister Lord Melborne, her 'Uncle King's' 'approachability' and slackening of court

William IV by David Wilkie, c.1837.
NATIONAL PORTRAIT GALLERY

etiquette, they agreed that although these habits had made William popular, the country required stricter and higher standards from a woman monarch.

After a reign which saw the passing of the Reform Bill, the abolition of slavery and the adoption by Belgium of a king friendly to Britain (Leopold of Saxe-Coburg, widower of George IV's daughter Charlotte), William's last days in 1837 were spent in bitter wrangling with the Duchess of Kent and her Controller, Sir John Conroy, who were determined to have control over the young heir to the throne. William was equally determined that they should not, by staying alive himself until Victoria had passed her eighteenth birthday on 24 May and could rule without a regent. William gamely survived until 20 June when, suffocated with asthma, he stroked the Waterloo Flag sent to his bedside by the Duke of Wellington and died gasping 'Glorious day . . .'.

LEFT *William IV as a young midshipman. Miniature by Jeremiah Meyer, c.1781.*
ROYAL COLLECTION

VICTORIA
Born 1819, reigned 1837–1901

When Victoria came to the throne as an eighteen-year-old in 1837 the monarchy had sunk low in public esteem, and her subjects regarded the young queen with sympathy mixed with gloomy foreboding, aptly summed up in Thomas Carlyle's pitying remark while watching her coronation: 'Poor little Queen, she is at an age at which a girl can hardly be trusted to choose a bonnet for herself; yet a task is laid upon her from which an archangel might shrink'. But at the end of her long reign Victoria had succeeded in transforming public opinion of the monarchy, largely by the force of her own personality. The robust shouts of 'Go it, old girl!' which greeted her appearance in her wheelchair on the Palace balcony for her Diamond Jubilee in 1897 epitomize the feelings of pride and loyalty which had come to be associated with the Crown.

Victoria's reign of sixty-four years was a unique period of peace for Britain. In Europe, the economic effects of the French Revolution and the Napoleonic Wars were profound and lasted well into the mid-nineteenth century. Britain, on the other hand, forged ahead with industrialisation, agricultural advances, the development of the railways, naval supremacy and empire-building, and the only two wars of the reign, the Crimean War in 1854 and the Boer War in 1899, were localised conflicts. As for empire-building, after the shocks of the Indian mutiny in 1857 the British Government, taking over from the East India Company, instigated a long period of sound administration in India. When Victoria, at Disraeli's suggestion, assumed the title of Empress of India in 1877, this move was greeted with general approval.

Throughout Victoria's reign enormous social changes were taking place at home, for although the Chartist movement was effectively crushed in 1848, almost all its demands and aims were realised within a relatively short space of time. The last two decades of the reign saw an increase in what was termed 'municipal socialism' – the provision of public libraries, museums, baths, parks etc., paid for and maintained from the

ABOVE
Queen Victoria. Oil painting by Sir Edwin Landseer, 1839, presented by Victoria to Albert before their marriage.
ROYAL COLLECTION

RIGHT
Queen Victoria riding out, with Lord Melbourne (right) and others. Oil painting by Sir Francis Grant, 1839.
ROYAL COLLECTION

Queen Victoria in Coronation robes. Oil painting (replica) by Sir George Hayter. NATIONAL PORTRAIT GALLERY

Prince Albert. Watercolour on ivory by Sir William Charles Ross, 1840. ROYAL COLLECTION

and music, was especially fond of dancing and enjoyed travelling; in 1843 the novelist Charlotte Brontë watched her passing through Brussels and was struck by her laughing face, and in 1855 Victoria found Paris the most beautiful town imaginable. A keen and skilful horsewoman, her 'ridings-out' in the first years of her reign, wearing her becoming black velvet habit, hat and veil, accompanied by a large cavalcade of companions, were one of the young queen's favourite pastimes. Always eager to try out new ideas, she was delighted with her first ride in a train in 1842 and soon the Royal Train was in use; and in 1853 she agreed to try chloroform during the birth of her eighth child, Leopold, and gave this disputed innovation her unqualified royal approval.

As for portraying the 'royal face', Victoria, herself a talented water-colourist and amateur etcher, was intensely interested in this aspect of monarchy, and was accustomed to sitting for artists from her nursery days. Her engagement in October 1839 to her cousin, Albert of Saxe-Coburg-Gotha, was the occasion

rates – and a surge of voluntary efforts to improve the lot of the urban poor.

The popular titles describing Victoria as the 'Great White Mother' of the Empire and the 'Grandmother of Europe', usually associated with the image of a sombre, unsmiling old lady submerged in widow's weeds, have tended to obscure her years as a very young wife, a mother and grandmother (she had nine children before she was thirty-six and was a grandmother at thirty-eight), her many interests and her zest for life. She loved theatre, opera

ABOVE *Queen Victoria, Prince Albert and five of their children (left to right): Prince Alfred standing, Edward, Prince of Wales (later Edward VII) beside the Queen, Princess Alice leaning over the baby Princess Helena, and Victoria, Princess Royal seated beside the baby. Engraving by Samuel Cousins from the oil painting by Franz Xaver Winterhalter, 1846.*
NATIONAL PORTRAIT GALLERY

RIGHT *Queen Victoria.*
Photograph by Roger Fenton, 1854.
ROYAL PHOTOGRAPHIC SOCIETY

Queen Victoria. Water-colour reproduction, made in 1883, by Lady Julia Abercromby of Heinrich von Angeli's state portrait of 1875. NATIONAL PORTRAIT GALLERY

for a happy exchange of portraits – she described Landseer's picture as 'the likest little sketch in oils of me that ever was done; en profile, the back seen, in my morning dress, without my tippet, and with my blue ribbon', and presented it to Albert before their marriage. When Victoria had to make her declaration of marriage with Prince Albert to her eighty-two privy counsellors, she wore a miniature of her fiancé by Sir William Charles Ross in a bracelet on her arm to help her through 'rather an awful moment'. Ross painted the couple many times, portraying the prince's good looks so vividly described by Victoria before her engagement: 'Albert really is quite charming and so excessively handsome, such beautiful blue eyes, an exquisite nose, and such a pretty mouth, with

delicate moustachios, and slight but very slight whiskers; a beautiful figure, broad in the shoulders and a fine waist; my heart is quite going . . .'. They were married in February 1840, and as their family grew, all its members were recorded in portraits by favourite painters including Robert Thorburn and, in particular, Franz Xaver Winterhalter who produced over 120 works for the queen.

His happy-family pictures, so much admired by Victoria that she copied his 1846 group in her private sketch-book, came to an abrupt end with the unexpected death of Albert in 1861. The Prince, aged forty-two, succumbed to an attack of typhoid. The harrowing scenes of Albert's last days, when the delirious prince wandered restlessly from room to room followed by the weeping queen and the helpless doctors, haunted Victoria for the rest of her life; not until February 1872 was she able to record in her journal the tragic beginning of her inconsolable widowhood. State portraits of the queen, henceforth, showed her royal face sorrowing but resolute. In 1875 Heinrich von Angeli, working on the official portrait, was worried that he was making his sitter look too earnest, only to be assured by the queen that a monarch should be represented with a serious expression. The Golden Jubilee in 1887 and the Diamond Jubilee in 1897 produced an enormous demand for prints, among them the immensely popular one by Sir William Nicholson showing the queen with her little dog.

Queen Victoria welcomed the invention of photography and patronised several well-known photographers, among them Roger Fenton who was instrumental in founding the Photographic (later the Royal Photographic) Society. Fenton produced many pictures of the royal family, although the stiffly-posed images cannot be said to add much to posterity's knowledge of the royal face. Victoria, however, evidently recognised the documentary value of the camera, by sending Fenton out to the Crimean War where he took nearly four hundred pictures and, on a later and personally sadder occasion, by having the Blue Room, in which Prince Albert had died, meticulously photographed to form a lasting record of this tragic event in her life.

Queen Victoria, who had presided over sixty-four years of momentous change and who had, in spite of general expectation to the contrary, established the constitutional monarchy firmly in the new age of democracy, died on 22 January 1901 at Osborne House. Lying supported in the arms of her grandson William, the German Kaiser, and her doctor, she drifted away as her family stood around her calling out their names. The final work of portraiture of the reign was depicted by the artist Emil Fuchs, who had produced many medals for the queen. Summoned to Osborne House, he made a series of drawings of Victoria on her lily-strewn deathbed, sleeping peacefully for eternity under her wedding-veil.

ABOVE *Queen Victoria with her little dog. Print from woodcut by Sir William Nicholson, produced for Victoria's Diamond Jubilee in 1897.* NATIONAL PORTRAIT GALLERY

ABOVE RIGHT *Queen Victoria with an Indian attendant, working on state papers out-of-doors, 1893.* NATIONAL PORTRAIT GALLERY

RIGHT *Queen Victoria on her death-bed. Charcoal drawing by Emil Fuchs, 1901.* ROYAL COLLECTION

EDWARD VII
Born 1841, reigned 1901–1910

Edward, the second of Queen Victoria's nine children and her first son, was born in November 1841 when his mother and father were both just twenty-two years old. Since 'Bertie', as he was called in the family, would in due course succeed to the throne, his education was of great concern to his anxious young parents. Many plans were formulated, but all were doomed to disappointment as the Prince of Wales was a reluctant scholar. Edward's relations with his mother were strained and uneasy, especially after his father's death for which Victoria felt he had been partly responsible (Edward

had indulged in a brief amorous escapade whilst up at Cambridge and Albert, already unwell, had travelled in very cold weather to remonstrate with his son). Matters improved in 1863 when Edward married the eighteen-year-old Princess Alexandra, daughter of the King of Denmark, a union of which Victoria wholeheartedly approved. Alexandra bore Edward five children between 1864 and 1869, two boys, Albert Victor and George (later George V) and three daughters, and became Victoria's favourite daughter-in-law. Edward, too, was slowly regaining his place in his

mother's affections. His serious attack of typhoid fever in 1871, when his life was despaired of, and Victoria sat by his bedside at Sandringham day and night, brought them together. The immense public concern and sympathy shown by the population as a whole during this crisis had the unexpected result of defeating republican agitation which was beginning to manifest itself, due partly to current ideas and partly to Victoria's secluded way of life since Albert's death. The queen realised the need to show herself occasionally in public and, at the Thanksgiving Service held at St Paul's in February 1872 to celebrate Edward's recovery, her dramatic gesture of raising her son's hand to kiss it was greeted with tumultuous applause.

For his part Edward, delighting in pomp and display, was absolutely cut out to be a public figure. Even his somewhat raffish life-style, his smart-set activities, his addiction to sport and gambling and his financial difficulties, which were always to be a source of anxiety to his

LEFT *Edward VII in Highland Dress. Photograph by Lord Redesdale, 1904.*
ROYAL PHOTOGRAPHIC SOCIETY

BELOW *Alexandra, Queen of Edward VII. Oil painting (replica) by Sir Luke Fildes, 1884.*
NATIONAL PORTRAIT GALLERY

mother, could not detract from his popularity. On the Continent, especially in France to which he paid frequent visits, Edward was a general favourite, and Victoria came to appreciate his cosmopolitan outlook. When, in 1901, at the age of fifty-nine, he became king (as the first and only monarch of the House of Saxe-Coburg, Albert's surname substituted for Hanover by Queen Victoria), he was very much a man of the world, practised in making public appearances and determined to bring the monarchy into the limelight of public awareness, a task he performed to perfection. In addition he had, during his long wait for the throne, prepared himself carefully as a democratic and constitutional monarch. If he lacked experience of politics he made up for it with his tact, charm and ability to get on with people, and in the field of foreign policy the *Entente Cordiale* with France in 1904 must be largely credited to him.

Sir Luke Fildes was chosen to paint the state portrait after Edward's accession in 1901. The king wrote after the first sitting: 'it promises to be good. I am represented in General's Full Dress uniform with the red velvet and ermine cloak life size . . .'. The coronation, fixed for 26 June 1902, had to be postponed until August of that year when Edward fell gravely ill and underwent an operation for appendicitis. John Singer Sargent, whom Edward considered one of the best portrait painters, never painted the king in life, but, summoned to Edward's death-bed in May 1910, he took the last likeness of the dead monarch. The Edwardian age, with its elegance and style, pursuit of pleasure and zest for life, and which concealed chasms of inequality, did not quite die with Edward VII in 1910; it continued in a feverish whirl for another four years, until the First World War was to bring about great changes which would prove the mettle of Edward's second son, who came to the throne as George V.

ABOVE *Edward VII on his death-bed. Charcoal drawing by John Singer Sargeant, 8 May 1910.* ROYAL COLLECTION

LEFT *Edward VII in robes of state. Oil painting (replica) by Sir Luke Fildes, 1902.* NATIONAL PORTRAIT GALLERY

GEORGE V
Born 1865, reigned 1910–1936

George V was forty-five years old when he came to the throne, having lived through thirty-six years of his grandmother Victoria's reign and nine of that of his father Edward VII. A second son, the unexpected assumption of the role of heir apparent on the sudden death of his elder brother Albert Victor, in 1892, was unwelcome to him; since the age of twelve he had been training for a career in the Navy for which he felt himself ideally suited and had received his first command in 1889. Naval habits of punctuality, discipline and attention to duty remained throughout his life and that, as king, he still felt himself to be a naval man is apparent in his reply to a request to show more geniality on official occasions: 'We sailors never smile on duty'.

That Prince George was able to support the role of heir willingly and successfully for the next eighteen years was largely due to his union with Princess May of Teck in 1893; arranged though this marriage may have been (Queen Victoria had destined the Princess for George's brother, Albert Victor, and had suggested the new alliance after the latter's death) it turned into an enduring love-match. On his own admission inarticulate, Prince George nevertheless managed to express his feelings for his young wife in a letter: 'when I asked you to marry me, I was very fond of you but not very much in love with you, but I saw in you the person I was capable of loving most deeply, if you only returned that love ... I know now that I do love you darling girl with all my heart, and am simply devoted to you ...'. The young couple represented Queen Victoria on official occasions, and were present when she died, Princess May lamenting: 'England without the Queen is dreadful even to think of', and her husband writing in his diary: 'Our beloved Queen and Grandmama, one of the greatest women that ever lived, passed peacefully away'. In 1901, after Edward VII's accession, the couple acted as his representatives on a long tour of Australia (where the prince opened the first Parliament of the Commonwealth) and Canada. In 1905 they visited India, returning there in 1911 for the Delhi Durbar Coronation after George became king.

George V's acquaintance with the Empire, his understanding of the role of the constitutional monarch, and his serious, conscientious and unpretentious assumption of the duties of the Crown, provided stability during the restless and unsettled age over which he reigned: through the ordeal of the First World War against Germany ('the war to end wars') when the name of the House of Windsor was adopted, the exhausted post-war years of the Depression, the first Labour Government of 1924, the General Strike of 1926, and the all-party 'National' Government of 1931 under Ramsay McDonald, up to the ominous approach of the Second World War.

The photograph was beginning to play a large part in royal portraiture and the increased circulation of newspapers brought royal faces into every home. Queen Mary (Princess May adopted this name on becoming queen) had travelled in Italy as a girl and was an art-lover throughout her life, collecting antiques,

LEFT
Queen Mary when Princess May, at Sandringham, 1897.
NATIONAL PORTRAIT GALLERY

BELOW
King George with Lord Stamfordham, working on state papers out-of-doors in the gardens of Buckingham Palace.
WINDSOR CASTLE, ROYAL LIBRARY

cataloguing the Royal Collections and specialising in the royal iconography of the descendants of George III, her great-grandfather. In general George V did not share his wife's interest in art, preferring his stamp collection, but on viewing with approval the group portrait of himself, the queen and their two eldest children in Sir John Lavery's studio in 1913, he wanted to have a hand in it and was encouraged by the artist to add a touch of blue to the Garter Rib-bon. George V, who had witnessed Queen Victoria's two Jubilees, and had grown up in the shadow of his formidable grandmother and his ebullient father, only became aware of his own popularity when his Silver Jubilee was celebrated in 1935 amid great rejoicing. After the death in 1936 of 'Grandpapa England' as his little granddaughter the future Queen Elizabeth II called him, nearly a million of his sorrowing subjects filed past his coffin as it lay in state.

Edward VIII was forty-two years old when he ascended the throne in 1936. At his birth in 1894, his great-grandmother Queen Victoria observed that never before in Britain had three direct heirs to the throne, as well as the sovereign, been alive simultaneously, a circumstance which produced many photographs and paintings on the popular theme of 'four generations'. The education of the prince followed the familiar lines of the Royal Naval College and Magdalen College, Oxford. But the outbreak of the First World War in 1914 had the student prince volunteering at once for active service. Taking a commission in the Grenadier Guards, he spent most of the war in the field, facing the same dangers as his men. The post-war years saw him fulfilling his role of future king by extensive tours of the Empire, promoting trade and confidence in the 'Mother Country', and of the mother country itself, inspecting social conditions.

ABOVE *Edward as Duke of Windsor. Study by Sir James Gunn, 1954.*
NATIONAL PORTRAIT GALLERY

LEFT *George V, Queen Mary and their two eldest children, the Prince of Wales (later Edward VIII) and the Princess Royal. Oil painting by Sir John Lavery, 1913.* NATIONAL PORTRAIT GALLERY

GEORGE VI
Born 1895, reigned 1936–1952

The four generations: photograph of Queen Victoria with (left) the Duke of York (later George V), (right) the Prince of Wales (later Edward VII), and the infant Prince Edward (later Edward VIII), 1899.
NATIONAL PORTRAIT GALLERY

Some eighteen months younger than Edward VIII, George VI had a similar upbringing to that of his brother, being sent to the Royal Naval College at the age of thirteen. At the outbreak of the First World War he was serving as a midshipman on HMS Collingwood. In 1916, in sick-bay on shore undergoing treatment for a duodenal ulcer, he insisted on returning to his ship to take part in the Battle of Jutland, of which he wrote a graphic account to his father: 'I was in A turret . . . the hands behaved splendidly and all of them in the best of spirits . . . my impressions were very different to what I had expected. I saw visions of the mast going over the side and funnels hurtling through the air, etc. In reality none of these things happened and we are still quite sound as before'. This experience made him one of only two British kings (or future kings) to take part in a naval battle; the other was his ancestor, William IV, who was at the battle off Cape Saint Vincent in 1797. He later took up flying, becoming the first member of the royal family to qualify as a pilot in the newly-formed Royal Air Force in 1919. In the same year he enrolled for a course at Trinity College, Cambridge.

When Edward VIII abdicated in 1936 the Duke of York (a title bestowed in 1920) experienced the same dismay as many of his subjects, but this was soon dispelled. In 1923 the Duke had married Lady Elizabeth Bowes-Lyon, daughter of the Earl of Strathmore, a marriage welcomed with delight by his parents. King George V had written to his son: 'The better I know and the more I see of your dear little wife, the more charming I think she is and everyone fell in love with her here'. When the young duchess became queen, she brought the same endearing qualities to her new position; the 'Royal Family' which included the couple's two little daughters, Princesses Elizabeth and Margaret, and not the solitary symbol of the king alone, became the image of a monarchy with increased prestige, a prestige enhanced during the testing years of the Second World War. The queen's brave words,

But the prince had fallen victim to the restlessness which had seized so many of his generation – refusing to marry and settle down to please his parents, his way of life caused them increasing anxiety. George V's gloomy prediction: 'After I am dead the boy will ruin himself in twelve months', ushered in his son's reign of less than a year. Opposed by British and Dominion Governments in his desire to marry Mrs Wallis Simpson, a twice-divorced American, Edward VIII abdicated after 325 days in favour of his brother the Duke of York, and accepted the title of Duke of Windsor. After serving as Governor-General of the Bahamas during the Second World War, he and the Duchess retired to France where he died in 1972, his wife surviving him until 1986.

The former Edward VIII and Wallis Simpson, wedding photograph by Cecil Beaton, 1937.
NATIONAL PORTRAIT GALLERY

on being urged to send her daughters to safety overseas: 'The children won't leave without me; I won't leave without the King, and the King will never leave', and on bomb-damage at Buckingham Palace: 'I'm glad we have been bombed; I feel I can look the East End in the face'; the king's quietly reassuring broadcasts (notably the inclusion in his 1939 Christmas message of some lines of Marie Louise Haskins' poem: 'I said to the man who stood at the gate of the year, "Give me a light that I may tread safely into the unknown"') which exactly mirrored his subjects' emotions; and the prompt royal visits to bombed cities (the king's broadcast on the outbreak of war had prepared his subjects for 'a conflict not confined to the battlefield') all served to strengthen the nation's feeling of solidarity with the royal family.

The changing post-war world of the last years of the reign witnessed the 1945 Labour Government, the granting of independence to India, Burma, Pakistan and Ceylon, the restructuring of the Commonwealth and the introduction of the welfare state. King George VI, in Winston Churchill's words, 'a model and a guide to constitutional sovereigns' died after illness in 1952 and was succeeded by his daughter who came to the throne as Queen Elizabeth II.

ELIZABETH II

Born 1926, reigned 1952–

Queen Elizabeth II came to the throne as a happily-married twenty-five-year-old and mother of two small children, at a time when, largely due to the efforts of her grandfather and father, the status of the monarchy was high. In these respects she differed from her two illustrious ancestors and fellow women-rulers, Elizabeth I and Victoria. Victoria, at eighteen a young, inexperienced and unmarried queen, had the hard task of restoring faith in the Crown; Elizabeth I took over a demoralised nation and throughout her reign was exercised with the problem of whether or not to marry. But in one important respect these three women monarchs may be deemed to be alike, in their highly developed devotion to duty. After her uncle's abdication and her father's accession in 1936, Princess Elizabeth grew up in the knowledge that she would one day have to assume the duties of the monarch. A child of thirteen when the Second World War began in 1939, she insisted five years later on 'joining up' like all other girls of her age, and entered the ATS (Auxiliary Territorial Service) as a subaltern undergoing training in vehicle maintainance.

Elizabeth's marriage in November 1947 to Lieutenant Philip Mountbatten, great-great-grandson of Queen Victoria (created Duke of Edinburgh on the wedding day), introduced her to life as the wife of a serving naval officer –

Prince Philip had joined the British Navy in 1939 and served in the Pacific during the war. King George VI's increasing ill health during 1951 made it necessary for his daughter to deputise for him on a number of official occasions. On 31 January 1952 the princess and her husband, representing the king, set off on what was to have been a long tour of East Africa, Australia and New Zealand, a tour which was tragically curtailed as George VI died on 6 February and his daughter flew home as Queen Elizabeth II.

BELOW LEFT *Queen Elizabeth II, when Princess Elizabeth, serving in the ATS during the Second World War. TR 2835.* IMPERIAL WAR MUSEUM

BELOW *Her Majesty The Queen, wearing the Ribbon and Star of the Garter and Queen Victoria's diamond and pearl diadem, and His Royal Highness the Duke of Edinburgh in the uniform of Admiral of the Fleet. Baron's Royal Command photograph, taken in April 1953, prior to the Queen's Coronation in June of that year.* CAMERA PRESS

OPPOSITE *Queen Elizabeth II. Oil painting by Pietro Annigoni, 1954–5.* CAMERA PRESS

As Queen of the United Kingdom and Head of the Commonwealth her duties and responsibilities are many and varied, including long tours – she is the most travelled monarch in Britain's history – and she combines this public role with the private one of wife, mother and grandmother. Speaking at the Guildhall Banquet held to celebrate her silver wedding in November 1972, the Queen told her appreciative audience the story of a bishop who, when asked what he thought of sin, replied simply that he was against it, adding that if she were asked the same question about marriage and family life, she would simply say: 'I am for it'.

The Queen's devotion to duty and her meticulous attention to the many tasks of the sovereign have set a standard already being followed by the royal faces of tomorrow. Her eldest son, Prince Charles, and his wife, Princess Diana, evince a serious and committed approach to social issues, participating, to an increasing extent, in the preoccupations and problems of contemporary society.

The Queen's happy family life has extended the unit of the royal family, in the public eye, to embrace her relations and, above all, her mother. The charming smile of Queen Elizabeth, the Queen Mother, caught in countless photographs, has given the public the eternal image, as enduring as Holbein's Henry VIII and Hilliard's Elizabeth I, of a royal face.

TOP LEFT
HRH The Prince of Wales and HRH The Princess of Wales, on a state visit to Cameroon, March 1990.
DAVE CHANCELLOR/

LEFT
HRH Charles, Prince of Wales, on his fortieth birthday.
DAVE CHANCELLOR/ ALPHA

ABOVE The wedding of Queen Elizabeth II's second son, Prince Andrew, Duke of York and Sarah Ferguson, 23 July 1986.
TIM BISHOP/TIMES NEWSPAPERS

TOP RIGHT
HRH Diana, Princess of Wales, with her two sons Henry (left) and William (right), outside the palace

of King Juan Carlos of Spain. Photograph taken during a family holiday to Majorca, August 1987. JIM BENNETT/ ALPHA

OPPOSITE
Queen Elizabeth, The Queen Mother on her seventieth birthday, 4 August 1970. Photograph by Cecil Beaton. CAMERA PRESS

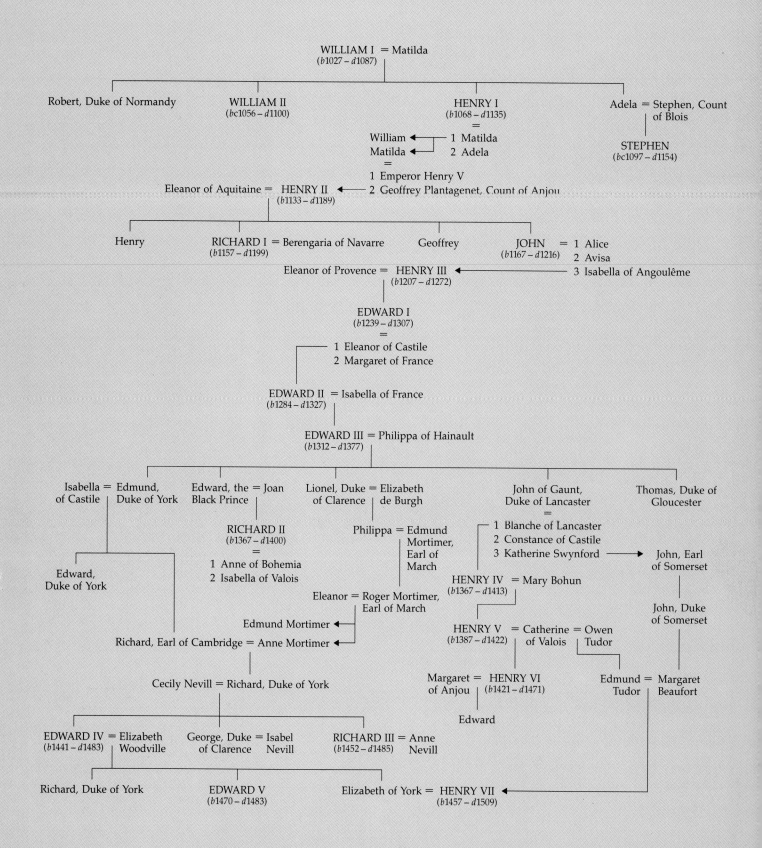

WILLIAM I = Matilda
(*b*1027 – *d*1087)

Robert, Duke of Normandy   WILLIAM II
(*bc*1056 – *d*1100)   HENRY I
(*b*1068 – *d*1135)
=   Adela = Stephen, Count
of Blois

William ← 1 Matilda
Matilda ← 2 Adela   STEPHEN
(*bc*1097 – *d*1154)

Matilda
=
1 Emperor Henry V
Eleanor of Aquitaine = HENRY II ← 2 Geoffrey Plantagenet, Count of Anjou
(*b*1133 – *d*1189)

Henry   RICHARD I = Berengaria of Navarre   Geoffrey   JOHN = 1 Alice
(*b*1157 – *d*1199)   (*b*1167 – *d*1216)   2 Avisa

Eleanor of Provence = HENRY III ←   3 Isabella of Angoulême
(*b*1207 – *d*1272)

EDWARD I
(*b*1239 – *d*1307)
=
1 Eleanor of Castile
2 Margaret of France

EDWARD II = Isabella of France
(*b*1284 – *d*1327)

EDWARD III = Philippa of Hainault
(*b*1312 – *d*1377)

Isabella = Edmund,   Edward, the = Joan   Lionel, Duke = Elizabeth   John of Gaunt,   Thomas, Duke of
of Castile | Duke of York   Black Prince   of Clarence | de Burgh   Duke of Lancaster   Gloucester
=
RICHARD II   Philippa = Edmund   1 Blanche of Lancaster
(*b*1367 – *d*1400)   Mortimer,   2 Constance of Castile
=   Earl of   3 Katherine Swynford → John, Earl
Edward,   1 Anne of Bohemia   March   of Somerset
Duke of York   2 Isabella of Valois   HENRY IV = Mary Bohun
Eleanor = Roger Mortimer,   (*b*1367 – *d*1413)   John, Duke
Earl of March   of Somerset
Edmund Mortimer ←   HENRY V = Catherine = Owen
(*b*1387 – *d*1422) | of Valois | Tudor
Richard, Earl of Cambridge = Anne Mortimer ←

Cecily Nevill = Richard, Duke of York   Margaret = HENRY VI   Edmund = Margaret
of Anjou | (*b*1421 – *d*1471)   Tudor | Beaufort

Edward

EDWARD IV = Elizabeth   George, Duke = Isabel   RICHARD III = Anne
(*b*1441 – *d*1483) | Woodville   of Clarence | Nevill   (*b*1452 – *d*1485) | Nevill

Richard, Duke of York   EDWARD V   Elizabeth of York = HENRY VII ←
(*b*1470 – *d*1483)   (*b*1457 – *d*1509)

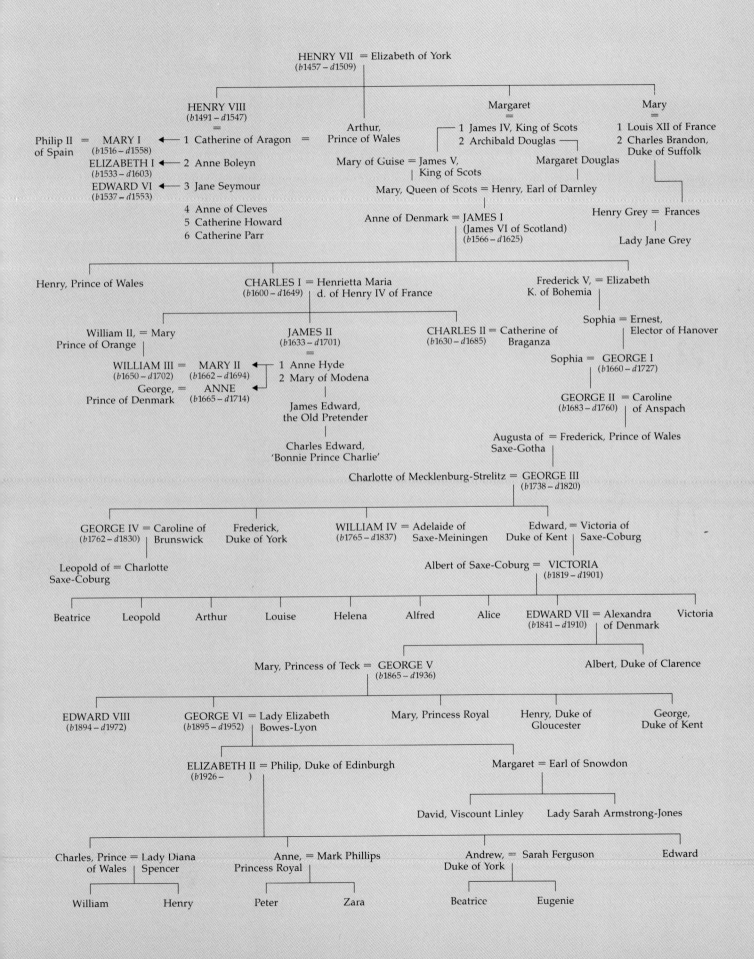

HENRY VII = Elizabeth of York
(b1457 – d1509)

HENRY VIII
(b1491 – d1547)
=

Arthur,
Prince of Wales

Margaret
=
1 James IV, King of Scots
2 Archibald Douglas

Mary
=
1 Louis XII of France
2 Charles Brandon,
Duke of Suffolk

Philip II = MARY I ← 1 Catherine of Aragon =
of Spain   (b1516 – d1558)
ELIZABETH I ← 2 Anne Boleyn
(b1533 – d1603)
EDWARD VI ← 3 Jane Seymour
(b1537 – d1553)
4 Anne of Cleves
5 Catherine Howard
6 Catherine Parr

Mary of Guise = James V,
King of Scots

Margaret Douglas

Mary, Queen of Scots = Henry, Earl of Darnley

Anne of Denmark = JAMES I
(James VI of Scotland)
(b1566 – d1625)

Henry Grey = Frances

Lady Jane Grey

Henry, Prince of Wales

CHARLES I = Henrietta Maria
(b1600 – d1649) | d. of Henry IV of France

Frederick V, = Elizabeth
K. of Bohemia

William II, = Mary
Prince of Orange

JAMES II
(b1633 – d1701)
=

CHARLES II = Catherine of
(b1630 – d1685) Braganza

Sophia = Ernest,
Elector of Hanover

WILLIAM III = MARY II ← 1 Anne Hyde
(b1650 – d1702) (b1662 – d1694) 2 Mary of Modena
George, = ANNE ←
Prince of Denmark (b1665 – d1714)

James Edward,
the Old Pretender

Charles Edward,
'Bonnie Prince Charlie'

Sophia = GEORGE I
(b1660 – d1727)

GEORGE II = Caroline
(b1683 – d1760) of Anspach

Augusta of = Frederick, Prince of Wales
Saxe-Gotha

Charlotte of Mecklenburg-Strelitz = GEORGE III
(b1738 – d1820)

GEORGE IV = Caroline of
(b1762 – d1830) Brunswick

Frederick,
Duke of York

WILLIAM IV = Adelaide of
(b1765 – d1837) Saxe-Meiningen

Edward, = Victoria of
Duke of Kent Saxe-Coburg

Leopold of = Charlotte
Saxe-Coburg

Albert of Saxe-Coburg = VICTORIA
(b1819 – d1901)

Beatrice   Leopold   Arthur   Louise   Helena   Alfred   Alice   EDWARD VII = Alexandra   Victoria
(b1841 – d1910) of Denmark

Mary, Princess of Teck = GEORGE V
(b1865 – d1936)

Albert, Duke of Clarence

EDWARD VIII
(b1894 – d1972)

GEORGE VI = Lady Elizabeth
(b1895 – d1952) Bowes-Lyon

Mary, Princess Royal

Henry, Duke of
Gloucester

George,
Duke of Kent

ELIZABETH II = Philip, Duke of Edinburgh
(b1926 –   )

Margaret = Earl of Snowdon

David, Viscount Linley   Lady Sarah Armstrong-Jones

Charles, Prince = Lady Diana
of Wales | Spencer

Anne, = Mark Phillips
Princess Royal

Andrew, = Sarah Ferguson
Duke of York

Edward

William   Henry

Peter   Zara

Beatrice   Eugenie

Printed in the UK for HMSO
Dd 291122   C150   9/90   63371